Rectrangles™

Pam Bono Designs, Inc.

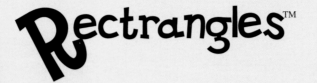

Rectrangles™

Published by

LEISURE ARTS®
the art of everyday living

LEISURE ARTS
5701 Ranch Drive
Little Rock, AR 72212
www.leisurearts.com

EDITORIAL STAFF

Editor-in-Chief:
Pam Bono

Editorial Assistants
Susan Clark, Nora Smith, and Robert Bono

Editors
Robert Bono, Susan Clark, Nora Smith

Art Director and Book Design
Pam Bono

Graphic Illustrations
Pam Bono

Photographer For Pam Bono Designs
Christopher Marona

Flat Shots By:
Jeff Laydon

Photographer For Zelda Wisdom
Shane Young

Photo Stylists
Christopher Marona, Susan Clark, Nora Smith,
and Pam and Robert Bono,

Photo Stylists for Zelda Wisdom
Carol Gardner and Shane Young

Produced by

Pam Bono Designs, Inc.

P.O. Box 659
Pagosa Springs, CO 81147
www.pambonodesigns.com

The information in this publication is presented in good faith, but no warranty is given, nor results guaranteed. Since we have no control over physical conditions surrounding the application of information herein contained, Leisure Arts, Inc. disclaims any liability for untoward results.

Copyright© 2005 by Leisure Arts, Inc. All rights reserved. This publication is protected under federal copyright laws. Reproduction or distribution of this publication or any other Leisure Arts publication, including publications which are out of print, is prohibited unless specifically authorized This includes, but is not limited to, any form of reproduction or distribution on or through the Internet, including posting, scanning, or e-mail transmission.

* Some products mentioned in this book may be trademarked, but not to be acknowledged as so.

Made in the United States of America.

Softcover ISBN 1-57486-441-6

10 9 8 7 6 5 4 3 2 1

Dedication:

To my husband, best friend, and partner for 39 years, Robert Bono. Thank you for introducing me to the two most valuable gifts that feed my creative soul: Colorado, and the beautiful music of Mr. Barry Manilow!

Credits

Designs by Pam Bono: Stars at Sea, Home For The Holidays, and Jingle Bulls Tree Skirt.
Designs by Pam and Robert Bono: Sampler Quilt.
Designs by Susan Clark: Clark Hybrid, and Prairie Stars.
Designs by Pam Bono and Susan Clark: Set The Table Place Mats, and Stained Glass. .
Design by Susan Clark and Robert Bono: Kodiak.
"Rectrangles" is a concept by Susan Clark and Robert Bono.
Quilting by: Mary Nordeng
Piecing by Susan Clark, Nora Smith, and Kim Zenk,
Binding by: Carolyn Matson

Special Thanks To:

Sandra Case and the art department team at Leisure Arts for being so great to work with.

Many, many thanks to Lorrie Bayger for her contribution of fabulous props for all of our books!

Joe and Carol Davis for so generously allowing us to invade your privacy for three days, move your furniture, and shoot beautiful photo's amoung the most impressive collection of early American antiques that we have ever seen. You are great folks!

John and Cheryl Nelson for allowing us to shoot in your elegant Victorian home. Special thanks to Kendall Nelson for a modeling job well done!

Cherron Adair owner of Adair Kennels, Aztec, NM. (505) 334-9834. Thanks for driving so far to share those adore-a-bull puppies!

Husqvarna Viking Sewing Machine Company for the loan of our Designer 1 machines.

RJR Fabrics, Benartex Fabrics, and Robert Kaufman Fabrics for your supply of lovely fabrics.

Carol Gardener, Shane Young and the fabulous "Ms. Zelda" for your participation in this book to add joy and laughter. www.zeldawisdom.com

My friends Pat Nicholas, and Wanda Nelson for your support and contribution to my creative side! Your years of friendship are valued.

The technique we are featuring in this book is not a new one, however we have found a way to use it with our other quick piecing techniques. As you can see, it can give a design a completely different look, and round off sharp points, giving the pieced design an appliqué look.

It is simplified so that templates are no longer necessary, nor must you go through the procedure of cutting the shapes; then trimming points, and finally matching triangular shapes to come up with a true rectangle.

The method that we have developed assures that points match, even though trimming is necessary only after the unit is made.

Rectrangles require practice, and I can not emphasize that enough. Some may be sewn using The Angler 2, while other larger Rectrangles require the drawing of a diagonal line, assuring accuracy. Pressing procedures are emphasized in our "Technique" section in the front of the book, and you will find that you have several pressing options, making the assembly of multiple units exceptionally accurate.

After practicing, so that the method becomes second nature, you will be amazed how easily the pieces go together and how accurate the matching of points can be. It produces beautiful effects that are easily achieved, even for beginners. You will find more graphics than usual in this book, leading you through the assembly of all Rectrangles visually.

Most of the projects in this book are designed to teach you how the method works by using traditional blocks as a starting point. You will notice the huge difference this method can make, particularly with the traditional blocks in our Sampler quilt. In testing the procedure, we found that blocks in the Sampler quilt were assembled within a 3 hour period. The people who pieced the blocks had never used the technique, and found it to be amazing how quickly the blocks went together.

Enjoy, my quilting friends!

Pam Bono

Table of Contents

Sampler Quilt. 14-59.

Prairie Stars Throw. 68-71.

Rectrangle Place Mat Set. 99-107.

Stained Glass. 92-98.

Learning Our Techniques

**The techniques shown on the following pages are used in projects throughout the book. Please refer to these techniques frequently and practice them with scraps.

STRIP PIECING

Strip Set 1. Make 2. Cut into fifty - 1 1/2" segments.

Strip piecing.

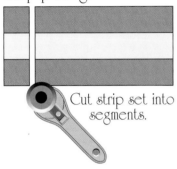

Cut strip set into segments.

For some projects, you'll join strips of different fabrics to make what is called a strip set. Project directions not only show illustrations of each strip set, but specify how many strip sets to make, how many segments are to be cut from each strip set, and the specific size of each strip and segment. In each project where strip sets are used, you are also shown exactly where to place them in the project diagrams and instructions. To sew a strip set, match each pair of strips with right sides facing. Stitch through both layers along one long edge. When sewing multiple strips in a set, practice "anti-directional" stitching to keep strips straight. As you add strips, sew each new seam in the *opposite direction* from the last one. This distributes tension evenly in both directions, and keeps your strip set from getting warped and wobbly.

DIAGONAL CORNERS

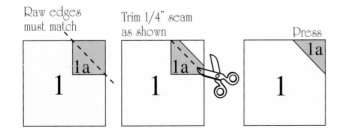

This technique turns squares into sewn triangles. It is especially helpful if the corner triangle is very small. It's easier to cut and handle a square than a small triangle. By sewing squares to squares, you don't have to guess

where the seam allowance meets, which is difficult with triangles. Project instructions give the size of the fabric pieces needed. The sizes given in the cutting instructions *include* seam allowance. The base is either a square or rectangle, but the contrasting corner is <u>always</u> a square.

1. To make a diagonal corner, with right sides facing match the small square to one corner of the base fabric. It is important that raw edges match perfectly and do not shift during sewing.

2. As a seam guide, you may wish to draw or press a diagonal line from corner to corner. For a quick solution to this time consuming task, refer to our instructions on the following pages for The Angler 2.

3. Stitch the small square diagonally from corner to corner. Trim the seam allowance as shown on the diagonal corner square only, leaving the base fabric untrimmed for stability and keeping the corner square. Press the diagonal corner square over as shown.

4. Many units in the projects have multiple diagonal corners or ends. When these are the same size, and cut from the same fabric, the identifying unit letter is the same. But, if the unit has multiple diagonal pieces that are different in size and/or color, the unit letters are different. These pieces are joined to the main unit in alphabetical order.

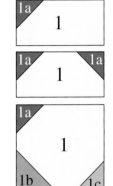

5. Many of our projects utilize diagonal corners on diagonal corners as

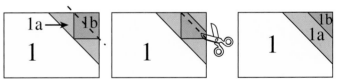

shown above. Diagonal corners are also added in alphabetical order. Join the first diagonal corner, trim, and press it out. Next add the second diagonal corner, trim and press it out as shown.

6. Our designs also utilize diagonal corners on joined units such as strip sets. In this case, the joined units will have one unit number in the center of the unit as shown at right. The diagonal corner will have its own unit number.

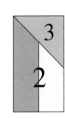

7. We have discovered many ways in which our quick piecing techniques can be used, especially with diagonal corners. See diagrams on the following page. Practicing these techniques so they become second nature to you, speeds you through a project, and will save a great deal of time.

IMPORTANT: If your diagonal corner is a light color on top of a darker fabric, DO NOT trim the center seam, or the darker fabric will show through!

Strip sets used as diagonal corners.

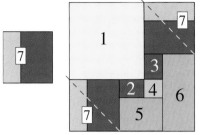

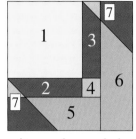

We have discovered how quickly units can be made by sewing together two strips of specified dimensions, then using these units as diagonal corners. This technique is very effective. To end up with horizongal stripes, Unit 7 is placed on the main unit with the stripes going vertically. To end up with vertical stripes, place Unit 7 on the main unit with the stripes going horizontally. Raw edges must match. Accuracy in piecing is critical to the final dimensions of a block. Stitch a diagonal seam as shown for both. Trim center seam and press.

DIAGONAL CORNERS USING THE ANGLER 2™

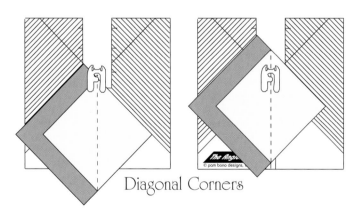

Diagonal Corners

When using the Angler 2, watch the point of your fabric on the center line - NOT the needle!

1. Align the diagonal corners with raw edges matching. Line the fabric up so the right side of the square is aligned with the first 45° line on the right of the Angler 2. Have the tip of the fabric under the needle. No seam guide lines will need to be drawn unless the square is larger than 7 3/4". As the feed dogs pull the fabric through the machine, keep the fabric aligned with the diagonal lines on the right until the center line of the Angler 2 bottom is visible. Keep the tip of the square on this line as the diagonal corner is fed through the machine. Trim the seam.

Multiple units using the diagonal corner and triangle-square techniques.

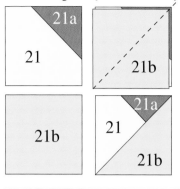

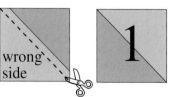

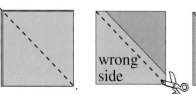

When you want two different 45° angles in the same unit, this technique works like a dream. First a diagonal corner is sewn as shown above; then our triangle-square technique is used to make this multiple unit.

TRIANGLE SQUARES

1. Many patchwork designs are made by joining two contrasting triangles to make a square. Many people use the grid method when dozens of triangles are required in a design. However, for the designs in this book we use a simple way to make one or more triangle-squares.
To do so, draw or press a diagonal line from corner to corner on the back of the lightest colored square.

2. As an extra tip, we have found that spraying the fabric with spray starch before cutting the squares to be used keeps them from distorting. A bit more fabric may be used; however, it is a quick and easy technique.

3. Place squares right sides together and stitch on the line. Trim the seam as shown and press. When you begin stitching these units, your needle may have a tendency to pull the tip of the square down in the hole. This is maddening! Our remedy is to use a small piece of stabilizer as a "leader", then follow with the diagonal seam. This technique may be done easily by using The Angler 2.

4. The illustration at right shows how triangle-square units are marked in the book. A diagonal line is always shown, separating the two fabric colors. The unit number is always shown in the center of the square.

7

Rectrangles™

The Rectrangle Technique!

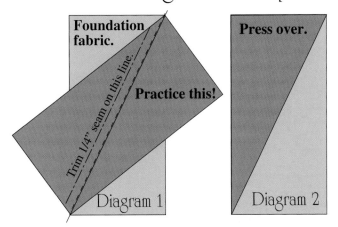

Foundation fabric.

Trim 1/4" seam on this line.

Practice this!

Diagram 1

Press over.

Diagram 2

Practice! Practice! Practice!

This is a wonderful quick piecing technique, which can be combined with our other quick piecing techniques. We do not suggest jumping into a project immediately, even though the first few projects are for beginners. Please read the instructions thoroughly and practice until raw edges match when the Rectrangle is pressed. It will not be long before the technique becomes second nature!

To Begin.....

Draw a diagonal line from corner to corner using a sharp pencil or a fabric pen that does not bleed. The solid line in the diagram is your drawn line. The dashed line is your stitch line, which is a threads width from the drawn line. The "scant" 1/4" is most effective when pressing, as it allows for take-up, and helps to assure accuracy. Trim on the dot/dashed trim line as shown.

Always trim on the side where the "scant" seam has been taken. Press Rectrangle over as shown in diagram 2. Do NOT trim the foundation fabric behind the top Rectrangle. If you have a light color in the Rectrangle, try to use it as the foundation piece, and place the darker fabric on top. If the lighter fabric is on top, when the 1/4" seam is trimmed, the foundation piece will show through.

Accurate cutting is necessary so that points will match as shown. Pin for larger Rectrangles so that the pieces and points do not move.

Pressing

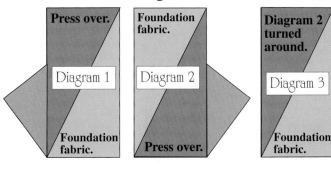

Press over.

Foundation fabric.

Diagram 1

Foundation fabric.

Diagram 2

Press over.

Diagram 2 turned around.

Diagram 3

Foundation fabric.

After the technique has become second nature for you, you will find that you may not wish to take the "scant" seam. In this case you will be stitching on the line that you have drawn. This gives you pressing options (before trimming) as shown. We have found that finger pressing in both directions, allows you to see which way the top Rectrangle is going to line up the best with the foundation fabric.

PLEASE NOTE: Once the diagonal is sewn, the angle will be the same, allowing you to press the top fabric in two different directions as shown in diagrams 1 and 2. The color will go in the same direction as shown in Diagram 2, by simply turning the piece around as shown in Diagram 3. The same applies if the angle is sewn in the opposite direction.

Before the angle is pressed over, we like to press the piece flat, right after stitching; then press the seam over on the side.

The Angler 2.
© pam bono designs, inc.

The Angler 2 may be used after the technique has become second nature. In order to see the center line the Rectrangles can not be larger than 1 3/4" x 3 1/2". For larger pieces, you may want to draw a "start line" on the Rectrangle itself so that The Angler 2 can be used. The "start line" should be drawn at least half way for accuracy, until the center line of The Angler 2 can be seen.

Trimming

Step 1   Step 2

Step 1 diagram:
Trim off 1/4"
1 1/2" x 3"
1a
1
1 1/2" x 3"
Trim off 1/4"

Step 2 diagrams:
1 1/2" x 2 1/2"
1a
1

1a
1
Seam Line

1. For Rectrangles, the length is always twice the width. As an example: 2" x 4".

2. Trimming off is necessary so that the points will match after the rectrangles are sewn into the blocks. It establishes your 1/4" seam allowance as shown in steps 1 and 2.

3. For all Rectrangle units, the first diagram will show the cut size of each unit. After trimming, the size that the Rectrangle should be will also be shown.

Trim off 1/4". Line ruler up so that unit is squared on end and one side.

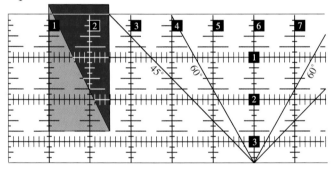

The finished size of what the unit should be when trimmed is shown in all of our project diagrams. Turn the piece around, and square it up once again as shown below. Trim off 1/4" on opposite end.

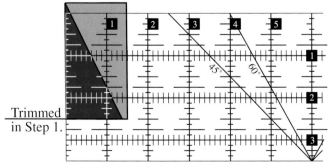

Another trimming option: Double Units.

After you feel that you have mastered the technique, double units as shown below may be joined together and then trimmed. To check the correct size the combined units should be after trimming, subtract 1/4" from the width of each unit; then add the two width measurements together. As an example, the units below are 1 1/2" wide x 3" long. Subtracting 1/4" from the width of each leaves a width measurement of 1 1/4" on each unit. The 1/4" is your seam allowance and will be sewn to join the units. Your total width should be 2 1/2" by adding 1 1/4" and 1 1/4". After trimming the 1/4" from top and bottom, your length should be 2 1/2" as you will subtract a total of 1/2".

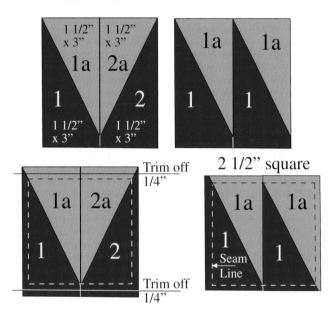

For Beginners

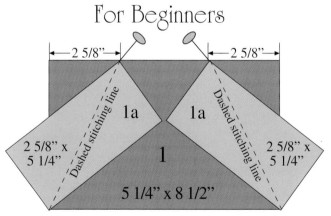

When practicing the technique, or doing your first project, we have marked the distance between the corner of the base fabric and where the point of the rectrangle should be. You may wish to mark the spot with pins as shown above. When you become more proficient, measurements will not be needed as swinging the points around will become second nature.

Adding diagonal corners.

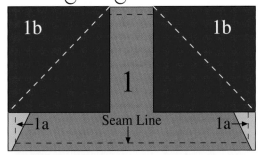

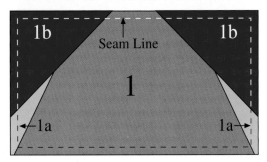

Diagonal corners are always added to Rectrangle units after they are trimmed. These units are added the same as for any diagonal corners.

Using Rectrangles as diagonal corners.

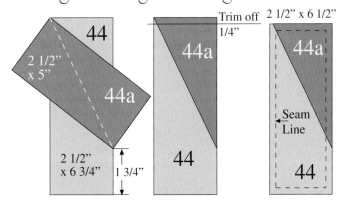

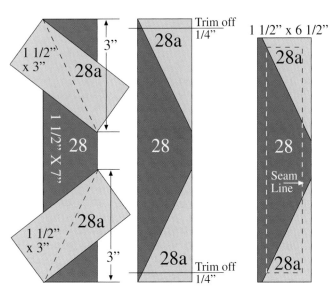

We have calculated the cut sizes needed for the base and Rectrangle units to use them as you would a diagonal corner. Again, measurements from base corners to Rectrangle corners are given as a guide. Only one side is trimmed as shown.

Double Rectrangle corners may be used as shown below. In this case, both the top and bottom ends are trimmed 1/4".

Quick Piecing Tricks!

MACHINE PIECING

An accurate, consistent 1/4" seam allowance is essential for good piecing. If each seam varies by the tiniest bit, the difference multiplies greatly by the time the block is completed. Before you start a project, be sure that you can sew a precise 1/4" seam allowance. Refer to instructions and illustrations for use of The Angler 2 in this section to aid with accurate seams.

1. Set your sewing machine to 12-14 stitches per inch. Use 100%-cotton or cotton/polyester sewing thread.

2. Match pieces to be sewn with right sides facing. Sew each seam from cut edge to cut edge of the fabric piece. It is not necessary to backstitch, because most seams will be crossed and held by another seam. We do back stitch the ends of the seams on the outer borders.

SEWING AN "X"

1. When triangles are pieced with other units, seams should cross in an "X" on the back. If the joining seam goes precisely through the center of the "X", the triangle will have a nice sharp point on the front.

CHAIN PIECING

1. Chain piecing is an efficient way to sew many units in one operation, saving time and thread. Line up several units to be sewn. Sew the first unit as usual, but at the end of the seam do not backstitch, clip the thread, or lift the presser foot. Instead, feed the next unit right on the heels of the first. There will be a little twist of thread between each unit. Sew as many seams as you like on a chain. Keep the chain intact to carry to the ironing board and clip the threads as you press.

Using Our Instructions....

The points on page 11 explain how the instructions in our book are organized. You will find that all projects are made easier if you <u>read this section thoroughly</u> and follow each tip.

• Yardage is based on 40-42" wide fabric, allowing for up to 4% shrinkage. 100% cotton fabric is recommended for the quilt top and backing.

• At the beginning of each project, we tell you which techniques are used so you can practice them before beginning. Seam allowances *are included* in all stated measurements and cutting.

• The materials list provides you with yardage requirements for the project. We have included the exact number of inches needed to make the project, with yardage given to the nearest 1/8 yard. By doing this, we are giving you the option to purchase extra yardage if you feel you may need more.

• A color key accompanies each materials list, matching each fabric with the color-coded illustrations given with the project directions. We have made an effort to match the colors in the graphics to the actual fabric colors used in the project.

• Cutting instructions are given for each fabric, the first cut, indicated by a •, is usually a specific number of cross grain strips. The second cut, indicated by *, specifies how to cut those strips into smaller pieces, or "segments." The identification of each piece follows in parenthesis, consisting of the block letter and unit number that corresponds to the assembly diagram. For pieces used in more than one unit, several unit numbers are given.

• Every project has one or more block designs. Instructions include block illustrations that show the fabric color, and the numbered units.

• Organize all cut pieces in zip top bags, and label each bag with the appropriate unit numbers. We use masking tape on the bags to label them. This avoids confusion and keeps the pieces stored safely until they are needed. Arrange all fabric colors, in their individual bags with like fabrics together, making it easy to find a specific unit and fabric color.

• In order to conserve fabric, we have carefully calculated the number of units that can be cut from specified strips. In doing this, units may be cut in two or three different places in the cutting instructions, from a variety of strips. So that cut units may be organized efficiently, the units that appear in more than one strip are shown in red on the cutting list. This immediately tells you that there will be more of that specific unit. Additional cuts are not only shown in red, but the

words "add to" are shown within the parenthesis so you may keep that zip top bag open, knowing in advance there will be more units to add. "Stack this cut" will appear frequently in the cutting instructions. Refer to the drawing below. We utilize the width of the strip with the first unit to be cut; then other units can be stacked on top of each other to best utilize the strips.

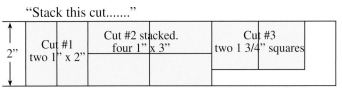

"Stack this cut......."

| Cut #1 two 1" x 2" | Cut #2 stacked. four 1" x 3" | Cut #3 two 1 3/4" squares |

2" wide strip. Do not cut strips down unless directed.

• Large pieces such as sashing and borders are generally cut first to assure you have enough fabric. To reduce further waste of fabric, you may be instructed to cut some pieces from a first-cut strip, and then cut that strip down to a narrower width to cut additional pieces.

• Cutting and piecing instructions are given in a logical step-by-step progression. Follow this order always to avoid having to rip out in some cases. Although there are many assembly graphics, we strongly suggest reading the written instructions along with looking at the graphics.

• Individual units are assembled first. Use one or more of the "quick piecing" techniques described on pages 6-11.

• Strip set illustrations show the size of the segments to be cut from that strip set. The illustration also designates how many strip sets are to be made, and the size of the strips. The strip set segments are then labeled as units within the block illustration. Keep strip set segments in their own labeled zip top bag.

• Each unit in the assembly diagram is numbered. The main part of the unit is indicated with a number only. A diagonal line represents a seam where a diagonal corner or end is attached. Each diagonal piece is numbered with the main unit number plus a letter: Example: (1a).

• Many extra illustrations are given throughout the projects for assembly of unusual or multiple units for more clarity.

MAKING DOUBLE SIDED NAPKINS

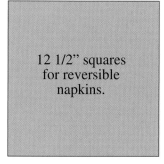

12 1/2" squares for reversible napkins.

Pieced or plain napkin.

Place right sides together with raw edges matching. Stitch as shown, and leave opening to turn.

Fold the napkin partially upwards to show both sides.

HELPFUL TIPS

All "Q" units in cutting instructions stand for "quilt top". These units are not incorporated into any specific block, however they are part of the quilt top.

HOW TO MAKE ONE BLOCK

Cutting instructions are given for making the project as shown. There may be times that you want to make just one block for a project of your own design. All you have to do is count, or divide if preferred.

With each cutting list there is an illustration for the block (s). Unit numbers in the cutting list correspond with the units in the illustration. Count how many of each unit are in the block illustration. Instead of cutting the number shown on the cutting list, cut the number you need for one block. Should you wish to make two or more blocks, multiply the number of units X the number of blocks you wish to make.

QUILTING TIP

The finished measurements for all projects in the book are given for the PIECED TOP. Quilting can take up anywhere from 1" - 3".
Be sure to take this into consideration.

Making a Flange Pillow

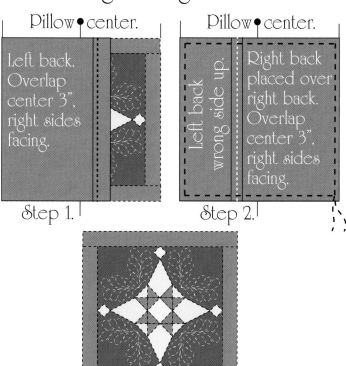

Pillow ● center.

Left back. Overlap center 3", right sides facing.

Step 1.

Pillow ● center.

Left back wrong side up.

Right back placed over right back. Overlap center 3", right sides facing.

Step 2.

Join borders to pillow top, and turn right side out. Top stitch through all layers around the inside of the borders, forming the flange. Insert 20" pillow form.

Straight-grain, French Fold binding.

Diagram 1
Joining binding strips.

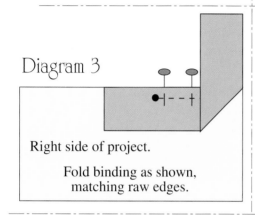

Continuous Binding
Bias or straight-grain.

Diagram 2

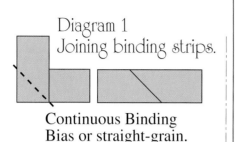

Fold binding in half lengthwise and press. Matching right sides, and beginning at lower edge of project, pin raw edges of binding to project, (dot) leaving a 6" tail. Continue pinning to within 1/4" of corner. Mark this point on binding. Use a 1/4" seam allowance and stitch to your mark. Backstitch at beginning of stitching and again when you reach your mark. Lift needle out of fabric and clip thread.

Diagram 3

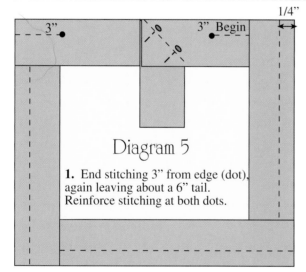

Right side of project.

Fold binding as shown, matching raw edges.

Diagram 4

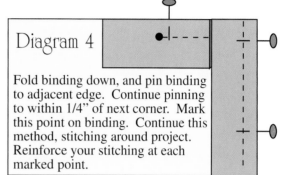

Fold binding down, and pin binding to adjacent edge. Continue pinning to within 1/4" of next corner. Mark this point on binding. Continue this method, stitching around project. Reinforce your stitching at each marked point.

Diagram 5

1/4"

3"   3" Begin

1. End stitching 3" from edge (dot), again leaving about a 6" tail. Reinforce stitching at both dots.

2. Fold left tail down at a 45° angle (perpendicular to top). Bring other tail straight across on top of folded bottom tail. Draw a 45° line from top left to bottom right where they meet, and pin in place as shown.
3. As there is plenty of room that is unsewn between the dots, pull the pinned binding out, and stitch the diagonal as shown on dashed 45° line. Trim seam 1/4" from stitching.
4. Complete sewing binding to project between dots, 1/4" from edge.

Back of project

Diagram 6

5. Trim batting and backing even with the seam allowance. Fold the binding over the seam allowance to the back. Blind stitch the folded edge to backing fabric. Fold and mitre into the binding at back corners.

Sampler Quilt

Each block of this beautiful quilt has been designed to take you through making your first Rectrangles along with our other "Quick Piecing" techniques. This could easily be the scrap quilt of your dreams! If you prefer to coordinate the fabrics as we have, complete yardage requirements for the entire quilt are shown below so that you may purchase your fabric for the quilt before beginning. The yardage requirements given include the blocks and sashing. Individual block fabric requirements are listed with each block.

Quilt finishes to: 84 1/4" x 110 1/2".
Techniques used: Rectrangles, diagonal corners, triangle-squares, strip sets, and diagonal corners on Rectrangles.

MATERIALS FOR ENTIRE QUILT

Fabric I (dark brown print)
Need 93"   2 3/4 yards

Fabric II (dark barn red check)
Need 23 1/2"   7/8 yard

Fabric III (barn red print)
Need 10 1/4"   1/2 yard

Fabric IV (dark rust textured print)
Need 39 1/2"   1 1/4 yards

Fabric V (dark gold print)
Need 35 3/4"   1 1/8 yards

Fabric VI (dark green print)
Need 38 1/2"   1 1/4 yards

Fabric VII (medium green print)
Need 61 1/4"   1 7/8 yards

Fabric VIII (light green print)
Need 44 3/8"   1 3/8 yards

Fabric IX (dark orange print)
Need 36 3/8"   1 1/8 yards

Fabric X (brown stripe)
Need 53 1/2"   1 5/8 yards

Fabric XI (medium gold textured print)
Need 19 1/4"   3/4 yards

Fabric XII (gold holly print)
Need 59 7/8"   1 7/8 yards

Fabric XIII (bright yellow/gold check)
Need 22 1/4"   3/4 yard

Fabric XIV (leafy tan print)
Need 41 1/2"   1 3/4 yards

Fabric XV (dark rust print)
Need 86 3/4"   2 5/8 yards

Fabric XVI (honey tan batik)
Need 45 7/8"   1 1/2 yards

Backing   7 7/8 yards

Shooting Star, Block 1

Block finishes to: 17" square.
Techniques used: Rectrangles, and diagonal corners on Rectrangles.

MATERIALS FOR BLOCK 1

Fabric I (dark barn red check)
Need 3 1/2"   1/4 yard

Fabric II (dark orange print)
Need 5 1/4"   1/4 yard

Fabric III (gold holly print)
Need 3"   1/4 yard

Fabric IV (bright yellow/gold check)
Need 5 1/4"   1/4 yard

Fabric V (light green print)
Need 4 3/4"   1/4 yard

Fabric VI (medium green print)
Need 3" x 5 1/2"   Scrap

Fabric VII (dark green print)
Need 3" x 5 1/2"   Scrap

CUTTING FOR BLOCK 1

FROM FABRIC I, CUT: (DARK BARN RED CHECK)
- One 3 1/2" wide strip. From this, cut:
    * Eight - 3 1/2" squares (C1b)
    * Sixteen - 1 1/2" x 3" (A1, A3, B1, B3)

FROM FABRIC II, CUT: (DARK ORANGE PRINT)
- One 5 1/4" strip. From this, cut:
    * Four - 5 1/4" x 8 1/2" (C1)

FROM FABRIC III, CUT: (GOLD HOLLY PRINT)
- One 3" wide strip. From this, cut:
    * Sixteen - 1 1/2" x 3" (A1a, A3a, B1a, B3a)
    * Four - 2 1/2" squares (A2, B2)

FROM FABRIC IV, CUT: (BRIGHT YELLOW GOLD CHECK)
- One 5 1/4" wide strip. From this, cut:
    * Eight - 2 5/8" x 5 1/4" (C1a)

FROM FABRIC V, CUT: (LIGHT GREEN PRINT)
- One 4 3/4" wide strip. From this, cut:
    * Four - 4 3/4" squares (Q1)

FROM FABRIC VI, CUT: (MEDIUM GREEN PRINT)
- Two 2 1/2" squares ((B4)

FROM FABRIC VII, CUT: (DARK GREEN PRINT)
- Two 2 1/2" squares (A4)

Block Diagram

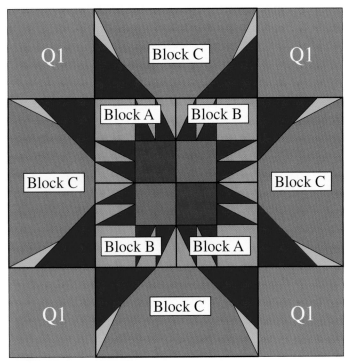

Block 1. Make 1. When completed, block should measure 17" square.

Assembly of blocks A and B.

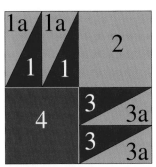

Block A. Make 2. When completed, block should measure 4 1/2" square.

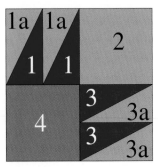

Block B. Make 2. When completed, block should measure 4 1/2" square.

1. For Step 1, units 1 and 3, draw a line diagonally from one corner to the other. Place rectrangles as shown. Use the Angler 2 (shown above) or stitch on the diagonal line. Pin if necessary so that the rectrangles do not slip.

2. For Step 2, press the top Rectrangle over as shown. Trim top Rectrangles even with foundation unit if necessary. Trim 1/4" off at the top and bottom of each unit as shown.

3. In Step 3, the diagrams show how the Rectrangle should look at top and bottom when 1/4" is trimmed off. The dashed lines on the diagrams show your seam allowance.

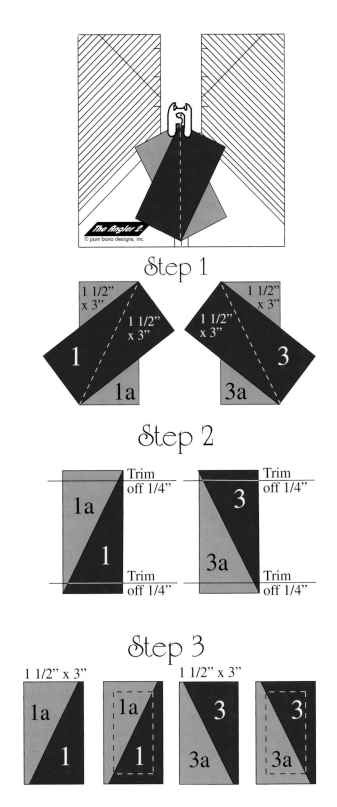

4. To assemble the blocks, refer to the block diagrams, and begin by joining units 1 and 3. Join Unit 2 to the right side of combined Unit 1's. Join Unit 4 to left side of combined Unit 3's.

5. Join the top and bottom section together, matching seams. Make two of each block.

Assembly of Block C.

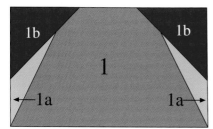

Block C. Make 4. When completed, block should measure 4 3/4" x 8 1/2".

Step 1

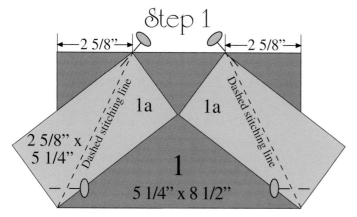

Draw a line diagonally on the rectrangles as shown. Measure in 2 5/8" from each top corner. Mark the 2 5/8" point with a pin and place one tip of the rectrangle at your mark. Bring bottom corner of Rectrangle, Unit 1a, to side edges of Unit 1 as shown. Pin them to keep them in place if necessary. Stitch a threads width on the outside edge of the stitch line. This gives you a "scant" 1/4" seam, so that when you press the rectrangle it will fold over and match the corners perfectly.

Step 2

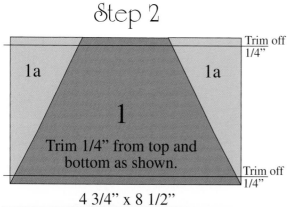

Trim 1/4" from top and bottom as shown.

4 3/4" x 8 1/2"

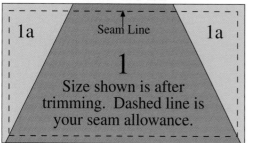

Size shown is after trimming. Dashed line is your seam allowance.

Step 3

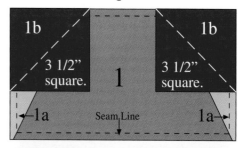

3 1/2" square.   3 1/2" square.

Seam Line

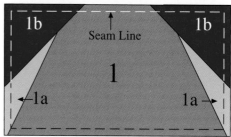

Seam Line

Join diagonal corner 1b as shown. Stitch diagonal, trim seam and press. Dashed line shows 1/4" seam.

Block Assembly

1. Refer to the block diagram, and join blocks A and B as shown for top of center section. For bottom of center section, join blocks B and A; then join the top and bottom sections together, matching seams.

2. Join Block C to opposite sides of center section, referring to block diagram for correct placement, matching diagonal seams.

3. Join Unit Q1 to opposite sides of the two remaining Block C's. Join the Block C/Q1 combined sections to top and bottom of block, matching corner, and diagonal seams to complete the block.

Whirly Gig, Block 2

Block finishes to: 17" square.
Techniques used: Rectrangles, triangle-squares, and diagonal corners on Rectrangles.

MATERIALS FOR BLOCK 2

Fabric I (dark brown print)
Need 9 1/4"   3/8 yard

Fabric II (dark orange print)
Need 4 5/8"   1/4 yard

Fabric III (medium green print)
Need 4 5/8"   1/4 yard

Fabric IV (leafy tan print)
Need 9 1/4"   3/8 yard

CUTTING FOR BLOCK 2

FROM FABRIC I, CUT: (DK. BROWN PRINT)
- One 9 1/4" wide strip. From this, cut:
    * Four - 4 5/8" x 9 1/4" (A1a)
    * Four - 4 5/8" squares (A3)

FROM FABRIC II, CUT: (DK. ORANGE PRINT)
- One 4 4/8" strip. From this, cut:
    * Four - 4 5/8" squares (A1b)

FROM FABRIC III, CUT: (MEDIUM GREEN PRINT)
- One 4 5/8" wide strip. From this, cut:
    * Four - 4 5/8" squares (A2)

FROM FABRIC IV, CUT: (LEAFY TAN PRINT)
- One 9 1/4" wide strip. From this, cut:
    * Four - 4 5/8" x 9 1/4" (A1)
    * Four - 4 5/8" squares (A2)

Block Diagram

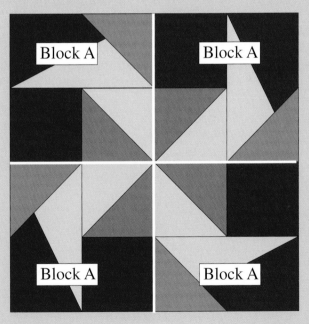

Block A   Block A

Block A   Block A

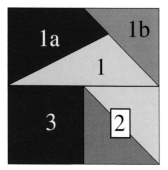

Block A Assembly

Block A. Make 4. When completed, block should measure 8 3/4" square.

Step 1

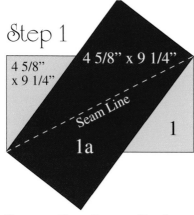

Draw a line diagonally from one corner to the other as shown. We use a chalk marker for dark fabrics. Place rectangles as shown. Stitch on the diagonal line. Make 4.

Step 2

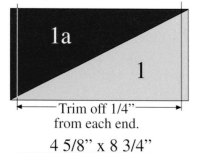

Trim off 1/4" from each end.

4 5/8" x 8 3/4"

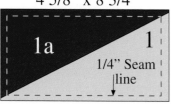

1/4" Seam line

Press the top rectangle over as shown. Trim off 1/4" at top and bottom. Unit will look like the unit above and will include your seam allowance, shown by the dashed lines.

Step 3

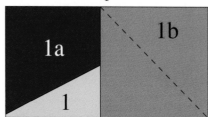

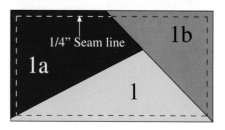

1/4" Seam line

Join diagonal corner 1b as shown. Stitch diagonal, trim seam, and press. Dashed line shows 1/4" seam line.

Step 4

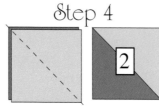

Place 4 5/8" squares of fabrics III and IV right sides facing, and raw edges matching. Stitch diagonal, trim seam and press.

Join units 2 and 3; then add these combined units to bottom of Unit 1 as shown in block diagram.

Block Assembly

1. Refer to the completed block diagram, and join the Block A's together as shown, matching seams, to complete the block.

Cross Roads, Block 3

Block finishes to: 17" square.
Techniques used: Rectangles,
triangle-squares, and strip set.

MATERIALS FOR BLOCK 3

Fabric I (dark brown print)
Need 8"   3/8 yard

Fabric II (med. gold textured print)
Need 6"   1/4 yard

Fabric III (medium green print)
Need 3"   1/4 yard

Fabric IV (dark gold print)
Need 1 3/4"   1/8 yard

Fabric V (gold holly print)
Need 1 3/4"   1/8 yard

Fabric VI (brown stripe)
Need 1 3/4"   1/8 yard

Fabric VII (leafy tan print)
Need 1 3/4"   1/8 yard

CUTTING FOR BLOCK 3

FROM FABRIC I, CUT: (DARK BROWN PRINT)
- **One 6" wide strip. From this, cut:**
  * Eight - 3" x 6" (A1a, A2a)
- **One 2" wide strip. From this, cut:**
  * One - 2" x 17" (Q2)
  * Two - 2" x 8" (Q1)

FROM FABRIC II, CUT: (MED. GOLD TEXTURED PRINT)
- **One 6" strip. From this, cut:**
  * Eight - 3" x 6" (A1, A2)
  * Four - 3" squares (A3)

FROM FABRIC III, CUT: (MEDIUM GREEN PRINT)
- **One 3" wide strip. From this, cut:**
  * Four - 3" squares (A3)

FROM FABRIC IV, CUT: (DARK GOLD PRINT)
- One 1 3/4" wide strip for Strip Set 1, Unit a

FROM FABRIC V, CUT: (GOLD HOLLY PRINT)
- One 1 3/4" wide strip for Strip Set 1, Unit b

FROM FABRIC VI, CUT: (BROWN STRIPE)
- One 1 3/4" wide strip for Strip Set 1, Unit c

FROM FABRIC VII, CUT: (LEAFY TAN PRINT)
- One 1 3/4" wide strip for Strip Set 1, Unit d

Block Diagram

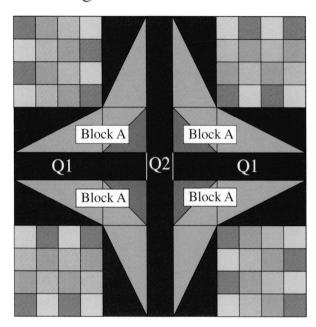

Making Unit A1

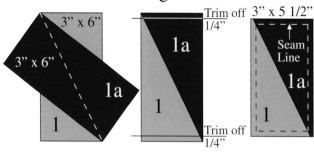

Refer to page 8 for Rectrangle techniques.

Making mirror image Unit A2

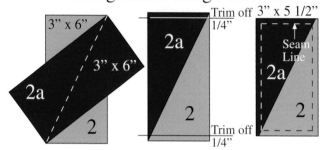

Block A Assembly

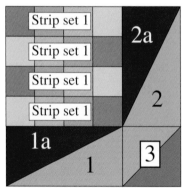

Block A. Make 4. When completed, block should measure 8" square.

Place 3" squares of fabrics II and III right sides facing, and raw edges matching. Stitch diagonal, trim seam and press.

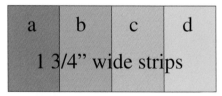

a	b	c	d
1 3/4" wide strips			

Strip Set 1. Make 1. Cut into sixteen 1 3/4" segments.

1. Refer to page 6 for Strip Piecing. The diagram above shows the strip set you are to make. Join the strips together and cut the segments as directed.

2. For Unit 3, refer to diagram and make four triangle-squares for Block A.

3. Refer to page 8 for Rectrangle techniques, and the diagram shown on top right. Make four of Unit 1 and four of Unit 2.

4. To assemble the block, begin by joining the strip set segments as shown in the Block A diagram. Make four of these strip set squares. Again referring to block diagram, join Unit 2 to right side of strip set square as shown. Join triangle-square, Unit 3 to Fabric II side of Unit 1 as shown.

5. Join the combined strip set square/Unit 2 to the top of combined units 1 and 3, matching corner seams.

6. Refer to the complete block diagram and join Block A to opposite sides of Unit Q1. Make 2. Join these combined Block A/Q1 sections to opposite sides of Unit Q2 to complete the block.

Tree Of Life, Block 4

Block finishes to: 17" square.
Techniques used: Rectrangles, and diagonal corners.

MATERIALS FOR BLOCK 4

Fabric I (dark brown print)
Need 2 1/4"   1/8 yard
Fabric II (dark green print)
Need 9 1/2" square   Large Scrap
Fabric III (medium green print)
Need 10"   3/8 yard
Fabric IV (dark gold print)
Need 6" x 8"   Large Scrap
Fabric V (med. gold textured print)
Need 10"   3/8 yard

CUTTING FOR BLOCK 4

FROM FABRIC I, CUT: (DARK BROWN PRINT)
- **One 2 1/4" wide strip. From this, cut:**
  * One - 2 1/4" x 5 1/4" (1)
  * One - 1 5/8" square (2a)

FROM FABRIC II, CUT: (DARK GREEN PRINT)
- One - 8 7/8" square (4) cut in half diagonally

FROM FABRIC III, CUT: (MEDIUM GREEN PRINT)
- **Two 5" wide strips. From these, cut:**
  * Twenty - 2 1/2" x 5" (5a, 6a, 11a, 13a)
  * Four - 1 3/4" x 3 1/2" (7a, 9a, 14a, 15a)
  * Two - 1 3/4" squares (8, 16)

FROM FABRIC IV, CUT: (DARK GOLD PRINT)
- One - 5 5/8" square (2)
- One - 2 1/8" square (3) cut in half diagonally.

FROM FABRIC V, CUT: (MEDIUM GOLD TEXTURED PRINT)
- **Two 5" wide strips. From these, cut:**
  * Twenty - 2 1/2" x 5" (5, 6, 11, 13)
  * Two - 1 3/4" x 4" (14, 15)
  * One - 3 3/4" square (17)
  * Two - 1 3/4" x 3 1/2" (7, 9)
  * One - 3 1/4" square (10)
- **Stack this cut:**
  * Two - 1" x 12 1/2" (12)

Block Diagram

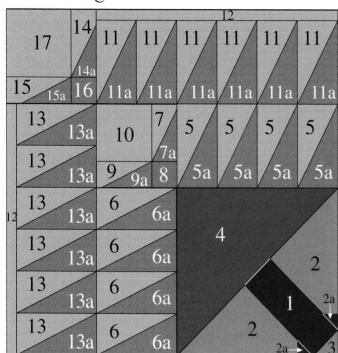

Step 3. Join triangle, (Unit 3) to bottom of tree trunk as shown. Trim to fit if necessary.

Step 4. Join tree top triangle (previously cut) as shown.

Step 3.

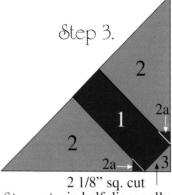

2 1/8" sq. cut in half diagonally.

Step 4.

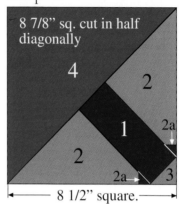

8 7/8" sq. cut in half diagonally

8 1/2" square.

Block Assembly

Step 1. Making the tree bottom.

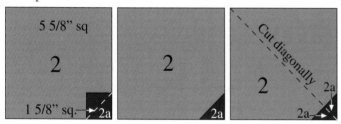

5 5/8" sq

1 5/8" sq.

Cut diagonally

Join diagonal corner, 2a. Trim seam and press. Cut the square in half diagonally as shown.

Step 2.

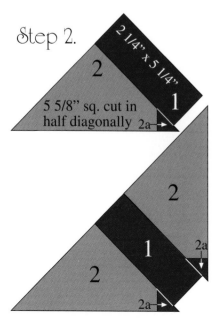

2 1/4" x 5 1/4"

5 5/8" sq. cut in half diagonally

Join one triangle (Unit 2) to side of tree trunk as shown in top diagram. Dark brown triangle will hang over 1/4".
Trim off even with trunk bottom. Join remaining triangle to opposite side of tree trunk.

Making mirror image units 5, 6, 11, and 13. Make four each of units 5 and 6 and six each of units 11 and 13.

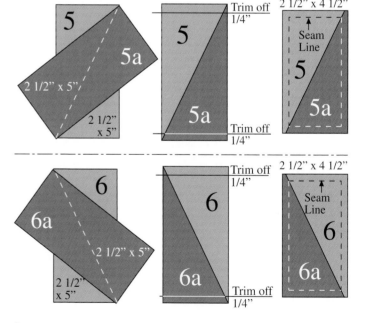

2 1/2" x 5"

2 1/2" x 5"

Trim off 1/4"

Trim off 1/4"

2 1/2" x 4 1/2"

Seam Line

2 1/2" x 5"

2 1/2" x 5"

Trim off 1/4"

Trim off 1/4"

2 1/2" x 4 1/2"

Seam Line

1. Draw a line diagonally from one corner to the other on the top Rectrangle. Place Rectrangles as shown. Pin if necessary so that the rectrangles do not slip. Refer to instructions beginning on page 8 for correct Rectrangle assembly.

25

2. Press the top Rectrangle over as shown. Trim seam even with Rectrangle; then trim 1/4" off at the top and bottom of each unit.

3. The Rectrangle diagrams show how the Rectrangle should look at top and bottom when 1/4" is trimmed off. The dashed line on the diagrams on the right shows your seam allowance, and gives the correct measurement the unit should be after trimming. For units 7, 9, 14, and 15, only the bottom of the Rectrangles are trimmed as shown. For units 14 and 15, refer to page 10, using Rectrangles as diagonal corners.

4. To assemble the block, begin by following the graphics and instructions to put the tree bottom together so that it measures an 8 1/2" square after it is sewn.

5. After all Rectrangle units are made, refer to the block diagram and begin by joining Unit 5 Rectrangles as shown. Join four. Join Rectrangles, Unit 6 in a row of four as shown. Join units 7 and 8. Join units 9 and 10. Join the combined 7-8 units to the right side of the 9-10 combined units as shown.

6. Join the row of Unit 5 rectrangles to the top of the tree bottom square. Press seams towards the darker fabric. Join the Unit 6 Rectrangles to the bottom of the combined 7-10 units, checking block diagram for correct placement. Join the 6-10 combined units to the left side of the tree, matching the corner seams.

7. Refer once again to the block diagram, and join six of Rectrangle Unit 11 as shown; then join Unit 12 across the top of the combined Unit 11's. Repeat this procedure with Rectrangle Units 13; then add Unit 12 across the top as shown. Join the row of Rectrangle combined units 11-12 to the top of the tree block.

8. Join units 14 and 16. Join units 15 and 17 as shown. Join these combined units together; then add the row of combined units 12-13 to the bottom of combined units 14-17. Join this row to the left side of the tree, matching corner seams to complete the block.

Making mirror image units 7, and 9. Make one of each.

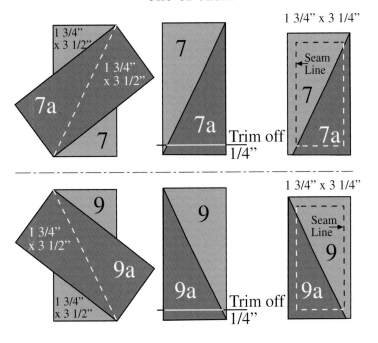

Making mirror image units 14, and 15. Make one of each.

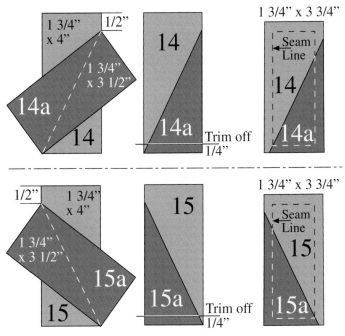

Fish Tails, Block 5

Block finishes to: 17" square.
Techniques used: Rectrangles.

CUTTING FOR BLOCK 5

FROM FABRIC I, CUT: (DARK BROWN PRINT)
- One 4" wide strip. From this, cut:
  * Sixteen - 2" x 4" (A1, A4)
- Two 1 1/4" wide strips. From these, cut:
  * Four - 1 1/4" x 8 3/4" (A7)
  * Four - 1 1/4" x 6 1/2" (A6)

FROM FABRIC II, CUT: (DARK RUST TEXTURED PRINT)
- One 3 1/2" wide strip. From this, cut:
  * Four - 3 1/2" squares (A3)
  * Four - 2" squares (A9)

FROM FABRIC III, CUT: (MED. GREEN PRINT)
- One 3 1/2" wide strip. From this, cut:
  * Four - 3 1/2" squares (A2)

FROM FABRIC IV, CUT: (LT. GREEN PRINT)
- One 4" wide strip. From this, cut:
  * Sixteen - 2" x 4" (A1a, A4a)

FROM FABRIC V, CUT: (GOLD HOLLY PRINT)
- One 2" wide strip. From this, cut:
  * Four - 2" x 7 1/4" (A8)

FROM FABRIC VI, CUT: (BRIGHT YELLOW/GOLD CHECK)
- One 2" wide strip. From this, cut:
  * Four - 2" x 6 1/2" (A5)

MATERIALS FOR BLOCK 5

Fabric I (dark brown print)
Need 6 1/2"   1/4 yard
Fabric II (dk. rust tex. print)
Need 3 1/2"   1/4 yard
Fabric III (med. green print)
Need 3 1/2"   1/4 yard
Fabric IV (light green print)
Need 4"   1/4 yard
Fabric V (gold holly print)
Need 2"   1/8 yard
Fabric VI (bright yellow/gold check)
Need 2"   1/8 yard

Block Diagram

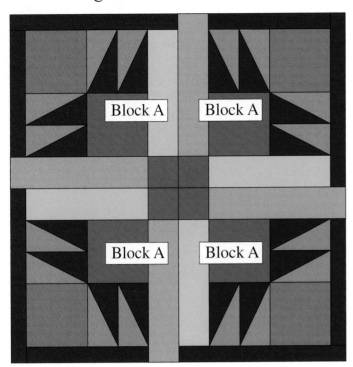

Making mirror image units 1 and 4. Make eight of each.

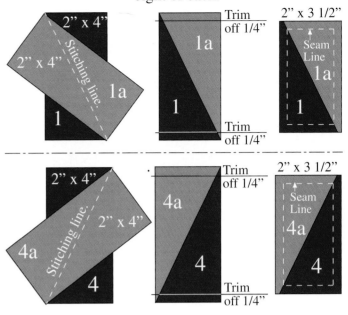

Block A Assembly

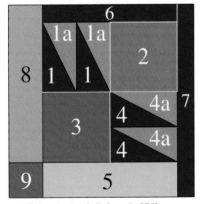

Block A. Make 4. When completed, block should measure 8 3/4" square.

1. Draw a line diagonally from one corner to the other on the top Rectrangle. Place Rectrangles as shown. Pin if necessary so that the rectrangles do not slip. Refer to instructions beginning on page 8 for correct Rectrangle assembly. Make eight of Unit 1, and eight of Unit 4.

2. To assemble the block, refer to the Block A diagram on the left. Begin by joining a pair of Unit 1's. Make four pairs. Join a pair of Unit 4's. Make four pairs.

3. Join Unit 2 to right side of the Unit 1 pair. Join the Unit 4 pair to the right side of Unit 3 as shown. Join the 1-3 combined units to the top of the 3-4 combined units, matching corner seams. Join Unit 5 to the bottom of the block; then add Unit 6 to the top.

4. Join units 8 and 9; then add them to the left side of the block, matching corner seams. Join Unit 7 to the right side to complete the block. Make four.

5. Refer to the Block Diagram, and join the four Block A's together as shown, matching seams to complete the block.

Cat's Cradle, Block 6

Block finishes to: 17" square.
Techniques used: Rectrangles, triangle-squares and Rectrangles as diagonal corners.

MATERIALS FOR BLOCK 6

- **Fabric I (dark brown print)**
  Need 4" x 7"   Scrap
- **Fabric II (brown stripe)**
  Need 8 3/4"   3/8 yard
- **Fabric III (dk. rust textured print)**
  Need 9 3/4"   3/8 yard
- **Fabric IV (med. gold textured print)**
  Need 3 1/4"   1/4 yard
- **Fabric V (leafy tan print)**
  Need 3 1/4"   1/4 yard
- **Fabric VI (medium green print)**
  Need 4" x 7"   Scrap

Block Diagram

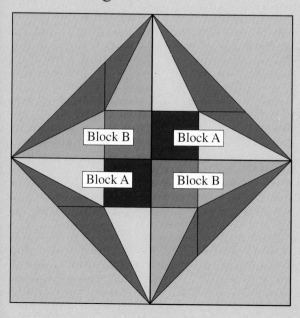

CUTTING FOR BLOCK 6

FROM FABRIC I, CUT: (DARK BROWN PRINT)
- Two - 3 1/4" squares (A2)

FROM FABRIC II, CUT: (BROWN STRIPE)
- One 8 3/4" wide strip. From this, cut:
  * Four - 8 3/4" squares (A4, B4)

FROM FABRIC III, CUT: (DK. RUST TEXTURED PRINT)
- One 6 1/2" strip. From this, cut:
  * Four - 6 1/2" x 8 3/4" (A1, B1)
- One 3 1/4" wide strip. From this, cut:
  * Four - 3 1/4" x 6 1/2" (A3a, B3a)

FROM FABRIC IV, CUT: (MED. GOLD TEXTURED PRINT)
- One 3 1/4" wide strip. From this, cut:
  * Four - 3 1/4" x 6 1/2" (B1a, B3)

FROM FABRIC V, CUT: (LEAFY TAN PRINT)
- One 3 1/4" wide strip. From this, cut:
  * Four - 3 1/4" x 6 1/2" (A1a, A3)

FROM FABRIC VI, CUT: (MEDIUM GREEN PRINT)
- Two - 3 1/4" squares (B2)

Blocks A and B Assembly.

Instructions and diagrams are the same for both blocks. Refer to block diagrams for color changes.

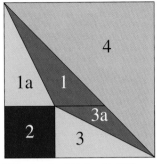

Block A. Make 2. When completed, block should measure 8 3/4" square.

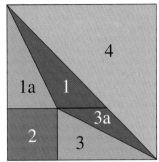

Block B. Make 2. When completed, block should measure 8 3/4" square.

Making Unit 3 for both blocks.

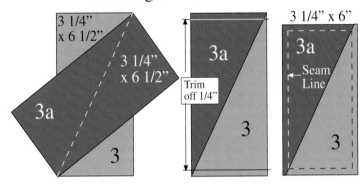

Assembly for both blocks.

Step 1.   ### Step 2

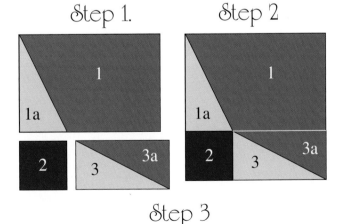

Step 3

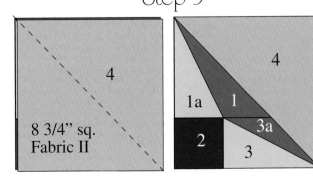

Making Unit 1 for both blocks.

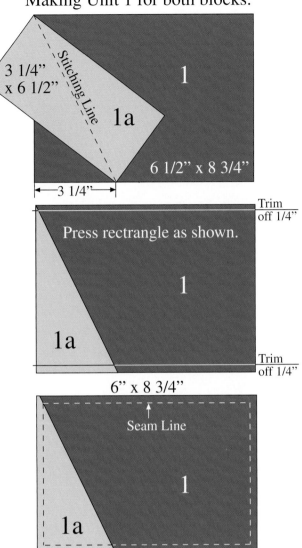

1. To make Unit 3, draw a line diagonally from one corner to the other on the top Rectrangle. Place Rectrangles as shown. Refer to instructions beginning on page 8 for correct Rectrangle assembly and pressing.

2. For Unit 1, place Rectrangle as shown above. Stitch diagonal line, trim as shown and press. Refer to block diagrams frequently for Unit 1a color changes.

3. For assembly of A and B blocks, join units 2 and 3; then add them to the bottom of Unit 1, carefully matching seams.

4. For Step 3, place Unit 4 over the top of completed block in Step 2. Place right sides together, and raw edges matching. Stitch diagonal, and press.

5. Refer to Block Diagram on page 29. Join the A and B blocks as shown, being careful to match all seams to complete the block.

In Bloom, Block 7

Block finishes to: 17" square.
Techniques used: Rectrangles.

CUTTING FOR BLOCK 7

▪ FROM FABRIC I, CUT: (DARK BARN RED CHECK)
- One 3 1/2" wide strip. From this, cut:
  * Two - 1 1/2" x 3 1/2" (A4)
  * Four - 3 1/4" x 6 1/2" (B8, B9)
  * Two - 1 1/2" x 4 1/2" (A5)

▪ FROM FABRIC II, CUT: (BARN RED PRINT)
- One 3 1/2" wide strip. From this, cut:
  * Two - 1 1/2" x 3 1/2" (B4)
  * Four - 3 1/4" x 6 1/2" (A8, A9)
  * Two - 1 1/2" x 4 1/2" (B5)

▪ FROM FABRIC III, CUT: (DARK GREEN PRINT)
- Two - 3 1/4" squares (B10)

▪ FROM FABRIC IV, CUT: (MEDIUM GREEN PRINT)
- Two 3 1/4" squares (A10)

▪ FROM FABRIC V, CUT: (DARK ORANGE PRINT)
- Four 2 1/2" squares (A1, B1)

▪ FROM FABRIC VI, CUT: (GOLD HOLLY PRINT)
- One 6 1/2" wide strip. From this, cut:
  * Eight - 3 1/4" x 6 1/2" (A8a, A9a, B8a, B9a)
  * Four - 2" x 6" (A7, B7)
- One 2" wide strip. From this, cut:
  * Four - 2" x 4 1/2" (A6, B6)

▪ FROM FABRIC VII, CUT: (BRIGHT YEL-LOW/GOLD CHECK)
- One 1 1/2" wide strip. From this, cut:
  * Four - 1 1/2" x 3 1/2" (A3, B3)
  * Four - 1 1/2" x 2 1/2" (A2, B2)

MATERIALS FOR BLOCK 7

▪ Fabric I (dark barn red check)
Need 3 1/2"   1/4 yard

▪ Fabric II (barn red print)
Need 3 1/2"   1/4 yard

▪ Fabric III (dark green print)
Need 4" x 7"   Scrap

▪ Fabric IV (medium green print)
Need 4" x 7"   Scrap

▪ Fabric V (dark orange print)
Need 5 1/2" square   Scrap

▪ Fabric VI (gold holly print)
Need 8 1/2"   3/8 yard

▪ Fabric VII (bright yellow/gold check)
Need 1 1/2"   1/8 yard

Block Diagram

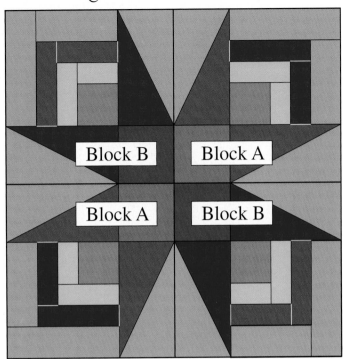

Block B Block A

Block A Block B

Blocks A and B Assembly.

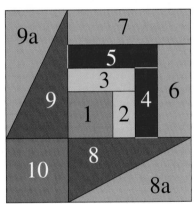

Block A. Make 2. When completed, block should measure 8 3/4" square.

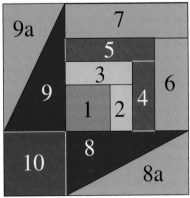

Block B. Make 2. When completed, block should measure 8 3/4" square.

Making units A8, B8

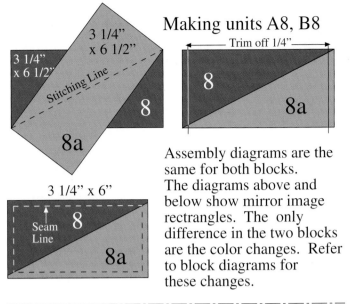

Assembly diagrams are the same for both blocks. The diagrams above and below show mirror image rectangles. The only difference in the two blocks are the color changes. Refer to block diagrams for these changes.

Making units A9, B9

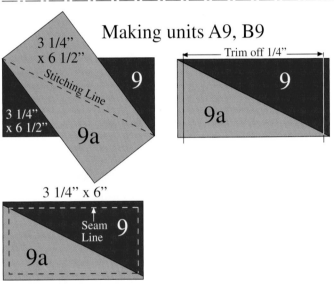

1. Draw a line diagonally from one corner to the other on the top Rectrangle. Place Rectrangles as shown. Pin if necessary so that the rectangles do not slip. Refer to instructions beginning on page 8 for correct Rectrangle assembly.

2. To assemble the block, refer to the block diagrams on the left. Assembly is the same for both blocks. The only difference are the color changes. Center assembly is a log cabin block. Join units 1 and 2; then add Unit 3 to the top of the 1-2 combined units. Join Unit 4 to the right side; then add Unit 5 to the top. Join Unit 6 to the right side; then join Unit 7 to the top.

3. Join Rectrangle Unit 8 to the bottom of the block. Join units 9 and 10; then add them to the left side of the block, matching corner seams. Make two of each block.

4. Refer to the Block Diagram, and join the A and B blocks together as shown, matching seams, to complete the block.

Stormy, Block 8

Block finishes to: 17" square.
Techniques used: Rectrangles, triangle-squares, and diagonal corners.

CUTTING FOR BLOCK 8

FROM FABRIC I, CUT: (DARK BROWN PRINT)
- One 4 1/4" wide strip. From this, cut:
  * Four - 4 1/4" squares (A6)

FROM FABRIC II, CUT: (DARK BARN RED CHECK)
- Two 2 3/8" wide strips. From these, cut:
  * Eight - 2 3/8" x 4 3/4" (A3, A4)
  * Eight - 2 3/8" squares (A1a)

FROM FABRIC III, CUT: (BARN RED PRINT)
- One 4 1/4" wide strip. From this, cut:
  * Four - 4 1/4" squares (A1)

FROM FABRIC IV, CUT: (DARK GOLD PRINT)
- Two 2 3/8" wide strips. From these, cut:
  * Sixteen - 2 3/8" x 4 3/4" (A2a, A3a, A4a, A5a)

FROM FABRIC V, CUT: (MEDIUM GREEN PRINT)
- One 4 1/4" wide strip. From this, cut:
  * Four - 4 1/4" squares (A6)

FROM FABRIC VI, CUT: (LEAFY TAN PRINT)
- Two 2 3/8" wide strips. From these, cut:
  * Eight - 2 3/8" x 4 3/4" (A2, A5)
  * Eight - 2 3/8" squares (A1b, A1c)
- Two 1 1/4" wide strips. From these, cut:
  * Two - 1 1/4" x 17" (Q2)
  * Two - 1 1/4" x 15 1/2" (Q1)

MATERIALS FOR BLOCK 8

Fabric I (dark brown print)
Need 4 1/4"   1/4 yard
Fabric II (dark barn red check)
Need 4 3/4"   1/4 yard
Fabric III (barn red print)
Need 4 1/4"   1/4 yard
Fabric IV (dark gold print)
Need 4 3/4   1/4 yard
Fabric V (medium green print)
Need 4 1/4"   1/4 yard
Fabric VI (leafy tan print)
Need 7 1/4"   3/8 yard

Block Diagram

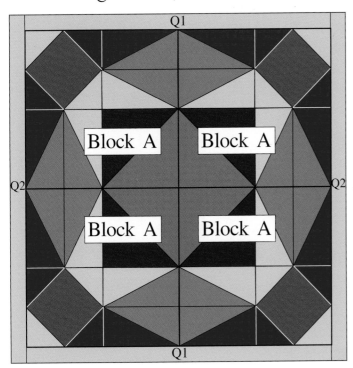

Block A Assembly.

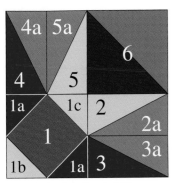

Block A. Make 4. When completed, block should measure 8" square.

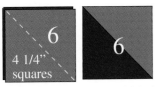

Place 4 1/4" squares of fabrics I and V right sides facing, and raw edges matching. Stitch diagonal, trim seam and press.

1. Refer to the block diagram at left and the triangle-square diagram. Follow instructions to make four of Unit A6.

2. For Rectrangles shown on right, draw a line diagonally from one corner to the other on the top Rectrangle. Place rectangles as shown. Pin if necessary so that the rectangles do not slip. Refer to instructions beginning on page 8 for correct Rectrangle assembly. Make four of each Rectrangle Unit. Use diagonal corner technique to make Unit 1.

3. To assemble the A block, refer to the block diagram on the left. Begin by joining units 4 and 5, matching points. Join Unit 6 to the right side of the 4-5 combined units. Join units 2 and 3

Making mirror image units 3 & 4

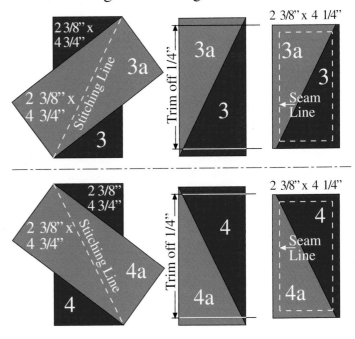

Making mirror image units 2 & 5

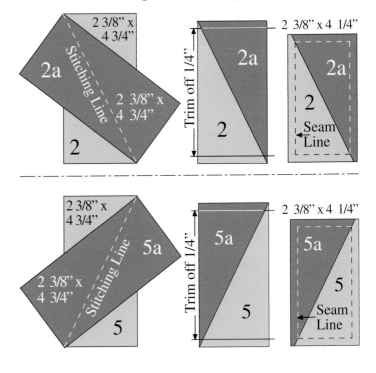

as shown; then add Unit 1 to left side of these combined units, matching points.

4. Join the top of the block to the bottom of the block, again matching seams carefully. Make 4 of Block A.

5. Refer to the Block Diagram above left and join the four A blocks as shown. Join Unit Q1 to top and bottom of the block; then add Unit Q2 to opposite sides to complete the block.

Diamond In The Cabin, Block 9

Block finishes to: 17" square.
Techniques used: Rectrangles.

CUTTING FOR BLOCK 9

◼ **FROM FABRIC I, CUT: (DARK BROWN PRINT)**
- **One 2 1/4" wide strip. From this, cut:**
  * Two - 2 1/4" x 7 1/4" (A6)
  * Two - 2" x 9" (A7)

◼ **FROM FABRIC II, CUT: (MEDIUM GREEN PRINT)**
- **One 2 1/4" wide strip. From this, cut:**
  * Two - 2 1/4" x 7 1/4" (B6)
  * Two - 2" x 9" (B7)

◼ **FROM FABRIC III, CUT: (DARK ORANGE PRINT)**
- **Two 2" wide strips. From these, cut:**
  * Four - 2" x 7 1/4" (A5, B5)
  * Four - 2" x 5 3/4" (A4. B4)

◻ **FROM FABRIC IV, CUT: (GOLD HOLLY PRINT)**
- **One 6" wide strip. From this, cut:**
  * Two - 3" x 6" (B8)
  * Four - 2 1/2" x 5 3/4" (A3, B3)
  * Four - 2 1/2" x 3 3/4" (A2, B2)

◻ **FROM FABRIC V, CUT: (BRIGHT YELLOW/GOLD CHECK)**
- **One 3 3/4" wide strip. From this, cut:**
  * Four - 3 3/4" squares (A1, B1)
  * Two - 3" x 6" (A8)

MATERIALS FOR BLOCK 9

◼ **Fabric I (dark brown print)**
Need 2 1/4"   1/8 yard

◼ **Fabric II (medium green print)**
Need 2 1/4"   1/8 yard

◼ **Fabric III (dark orange print)**
Need 4"   1/4 yard

◻ **Fabric IV (gold holly print)**
Need 6"   1/4 yard

◻ **Fabric V (bright yellow/gold check)**
Need 3 3/4"   1/4 yard

Block Diagram

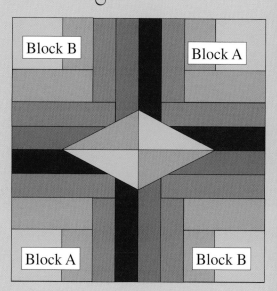

Blocks A And B Assembly.

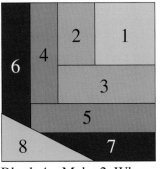

Block A. Make 2. When completed, block should measure 8 3/4" square.

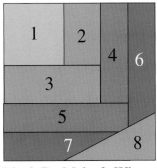

Block B. Make 2. When completed, block should measure 8 3/4" square.

1. To assemble the Log Cabin part of the blocks, join units 1 and 2; then add Unit 3 to the bottom of the 1-2 combined units. Join Unit 4 to sides of the 1-3 combination; then add Unit 5 to the bottom as shown. Join Unit 6 to the side; then add Unit 7 to the bottom to complete the log cabin. Make two of each.

2. Refer to the diagrams and instructions below for joining the Rectrangle corners. Complete instructions for Rectrangle units begin on page 8.

3. To complete the block, beginning at the top, join blocks B and A together as shown, matching the diamond seam. For the bottom, join blocks A and B together, again matching the diamond seam. Join the top and bottom sections together, matching diamond seams to complete the block.

Making Block A

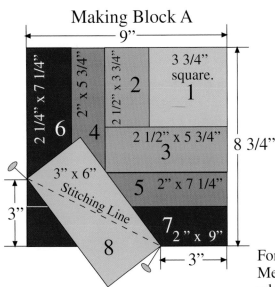

Trim off 1/4" on solid line.

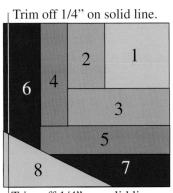

Trim off 1/4" on solid line.

8 3/4" square

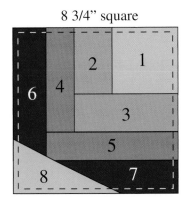

For A and B Rectrangles:
Measure up 3" on left side of block as shown. Measure in 3" from right edge as shown. Place pins for a guide. Place the Rectrangle as shown. Press Rectrangle and trim.

Making Block B

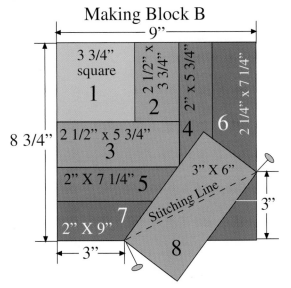

Trim off 1/4"

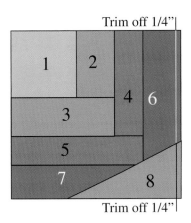

Trim off 1/4"

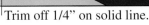

8 3/4" square

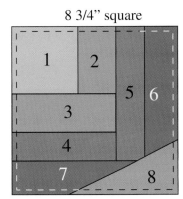

Pineapple, Block 10

Block finishes to: 17" square.
Techniques used: Rectrangles, diagonal corners, tringle-squares. and Rectrangles used as diagonal corners.

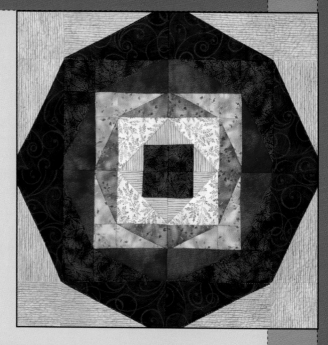

CUTTING FOR BLOCK 10

■ **FROM FABRIC I, CUT: (DARK BROWN PRINT)**
- **One 6 1/2" wide strip. From this, cut:**
  * Eight - 3" x 6 1/2 (A11, A12)

■ **FROM FABRIC II, CUT: (DARK GREEN PRINT)**
- **One 4 1/2" strip. From this, cut:**
  * Eight - 2 1/4" x 4 1/2" (A8a, A9a)
  * Four - 2 1/4" squares (A10)
  * Four - 1 7/8" squares (A1)

■ **FROM FABRIC III, CUT: (LIGHT GREEN PRINT)**
- **One 3 1/2" wide strip. From this, cut:**
  * Eight - 1 3/4" x 3 1/2" (A5a, A6a)
  * Four - 1 3/4" squares (A7)

■ **FROM FABRIC IV, CUT: (DARK RUST TEXTURED PRINT)**
- **One 2 1/4" wide strip. From this, cut:**
  * Eight - 2 1/4" x 4 3/4" (A8, A9)

■ **FROM FABRIC V, CUT: (DARK ORANGE PRINT)**
- **One 1 3/4" wide strip. From this, cut:**
  * Eight - 1 3/4" x 3 1/2" (A5, A6)

■ **FROM FABRIC VI, CUT: (BROWN STRIPE)**
- **One 6" wide strip. From this, cut:**
  * Eight - 3" x 6" (A11a, A12a)
  * Four - 3" squares (A13)
- **One 1 7/8" wide strip. From this, cut:**
  * Four - 1 7/8" x 3 1/4" (A3)
  * Four - 1 7/8" squares (A2)

■ **FROM FABRIC VII, CUT: (LEAFY TAN PRINT)**
- **One 3 1/4" wide strip. From this, cut:**
  * Four - 3 1/4" squares (A4)

MATERIALS FOR BLOCK 10

■ **Fabric I (dark brown print)**
Need 6 1/2"   1/4 yard
■ **Fabric II (dark green print)**
Need 4 1/2"   1/4 yard
■ **Fabric III (light green print)**
Need 3 1/2"   1/4 yard
■ **Fabric IV (dk. rust textured print)**
Need 2 1/4"   1/8 yard
■ **Fabric V (dark orange print)**
Need 1 3/4"   1/8 yard
□ **Fabric VI (brown stripe)**
Need 7 7/8"   3/8 yard
□ **Fabric VII (leafy tan print)**
Need 3 1/4"   1/4 yard

Block Diagram

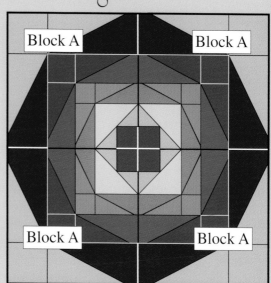

Block A   Block A

Block A   Block A

Block A Assembly.

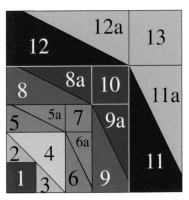

Block A Make 4. When completed, block should measure 8 3/4" square.

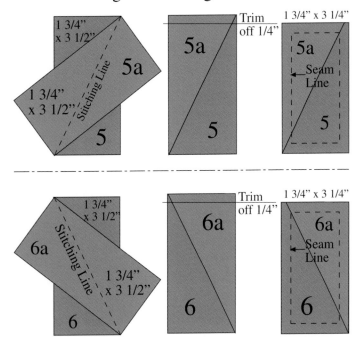

Join units 1 and 2; then add Unit 3 to right side of these combined units. Place 3 1/4" square of Fabric VII (Unit 4) right sides facing and raw edges matching on combined 1-3 units. Stitch diagonal, trim seam and press.

Making mirror image units 5 and 6

1. To assemble Block A, refer to the diagram for making units 1-4 and follow the instructions given.

2. Refer to the Rectrangle diagrams for joining the Rectrangles. Complete instructions for Rectrangle units begin on page 8. Make four of each unit.

Making mirror image units 8 and 9

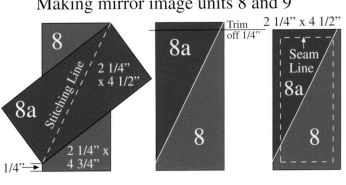

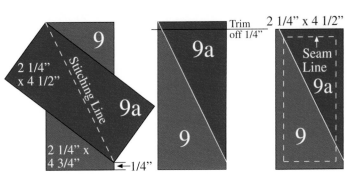

Making mirror image units 11 and 12

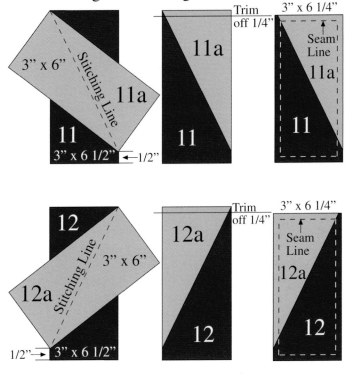

3. To assemble the block, refer to the Block Diagram above, and begin by joining Rectrangle, Unit 5 to top of center section. Join units 6 and 7; then add them to the right side of the center section, matching corner seams. Join Unit 8 to the top as shown. Join units 9 and 10; then add them to the right side of the block, again matching seams. Join Unit 12 to the top. Join units 11 and 13; then add them to the right side of the block, matching seams. Make four of Block A.

4. Refer to Block Diagram on page 37. Join the four A blocks as shown to complete the block.

Basket, Block 11

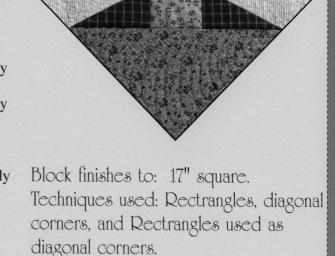

CUTTING FOR BLOCK 11

◻ **FROM FABRIC I, CUT: (BROWN STRIPE)**
- **One 6 1/2" wide strip. From this, cut:**
  * Two - 6 1/2" squares (20)
  * One - 5 1/4" square (14) cut in half diagonally
  * Two - 4" x 4 1/2" (7, 8)
  * One - 4 3/8" square (21) cut in half diagonally
  * Two - 3" x 4" (5, 6)
  * Two - 1 1/2" x 3" (18)
- **One 3 3/8" wide strip. From this, cut:**
  * Two - 3 3/8" squares (17) cut in half diagonally
  * Two - 2 5/8" x 2 7/8" (12)
  * Two - 2 7/8" x 5 3/4" (9, 10)

◼ **FROM FABRIC II, CUT; (DK. BARN RED CHECK)**
- **One 5 3/4" wide strip. From this, cut:**
  * Two - 2 7/8" x 5 3/4" (9a, 10a)
  * Two - 4" x 5 1/2" (15)
  * Twelve - 2" x 4" (1a, 3a, 5a and, 6a)
  * Two - 1 1/2" squares (19)
- **One 3" wide strip. From this, cut:**
  * Two - 3" squares (16)

◻ **FROM FABRIC III, CUT: (DARK GOLD PRINT)**
- **One 2 7/8" wide strip. From this, cut:**
  * One - 2 7/8" x 3 1/2" (11)
  * Six - 2" x 4" (2a, 4a, 7a, and 8a)

◻ **FROM FABRIC IV, CUT: (MEDIUM GREEN PRINT)**
- **One 9 7/8" wide strip. From this, cut:**
  * One - 9 7/8" square (13) cut in half diagonally.

◻ **FROM FABRIC V, CUT: (GOLD HOLLY PRINT)**
- **One 4" wide strip. From this, cut:**
  * Fourteen - 2" x 4" (1, 2, 3, and 4)

Block finishes to: 17" square.
Techniques used: Rectrangles, diagonal corners, and Rectrangles used as diagonal corners.

MATERIALS FOR BLOCK 11

◻ **Fabric I (brown stripe)**
Need 9 7/8"   3/8 yard

◼ **Fabric II (dark barn red check)**
Need 8 3/4"   3/8 yard

◻ **Fabric III (dark gold print)**
Need 2 7/8"   1/8 yard

◻ **Fabric IV (medium green print)**
Need 9 7/8"   3/8 yard

◻ **Fabric V (gold holly print)**
Need 4"   1/4 yard

Block Diagram And Assembly

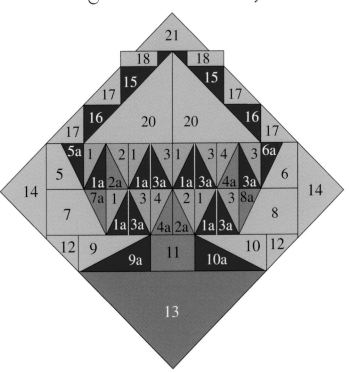

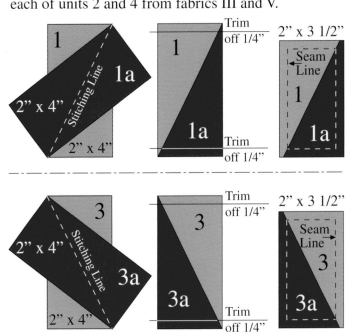

Making mirror image units 1, 2, 3, and 4. Units are made the same way, only the colors are different. Refer to Block Diagram for color changes. Make five of units 1 and 3, from fabrics II and V, and make two each of units 2 and 4 from fabrics III and V.

Making mirror image units 5 and 6. Make one of each.

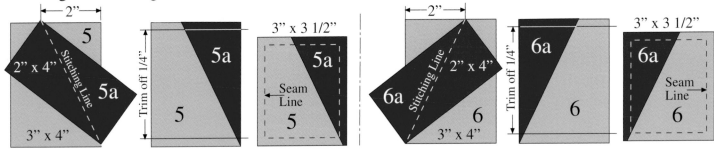

Making mirror image units 7 and 8. Make one of each.

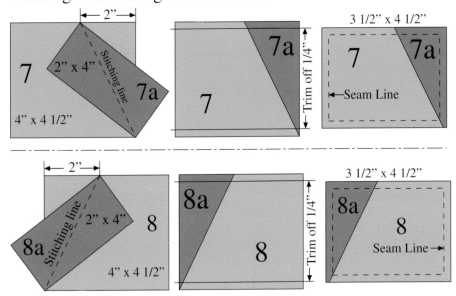

1. Basket Block A, is a series of Rectrangles and triangles. Once the Rectrangles are made, assembly is easy.

2. Refer to the diagrams for making the Rectrangles. Please read the instructions given with units 9 and 10 on the following page for correct assembly of the units. Complete instructions for Rectrangle units begin on page 8.

3. Refer to the assembly for the basket top on Page 41. Follow the instructions given to complete the handle of the basket.

4. For the basket bottom, begin by joining the top row of the basket, beginning from left to right join:

Making mirror image units 9 and 10. Make one of each.

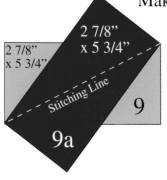

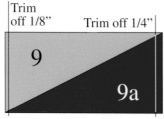

Please note: Look closely at the graphic above. 1/4" is trimmed from one short side, and 1/8" is trimmed from the other short side.

Please note: Circle and blow up diagram on left shows tip of Fabric I is 1/8" beyond the rectrangle.

Please note: Look closely at the graphic above. 1/4" is trimmed from one short side, and 1/8" is trimmed from the other short side.

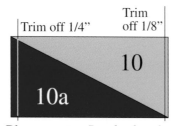

Please note: Circle and blow up diagram on right shows tip of Fabric I is 1/8" beyond the rectrangle.

Making combined units 15-21.

Step 1.

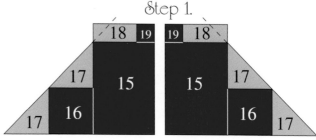

Join one Unit 17 triangle to side and top of Unit 16. Trim to fit. Join units 18 and 19; then add Unit 15 to bottom of the 18/19combined units. Join combined units 16/17 to side as shown. Trim Unit 18 even with Units 17 as shown with dashed line.

Step 2.

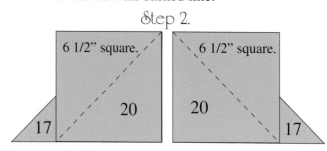

Place 6 1/2" square of Fabric I on top of combined 16-19 units with bottom and side raw edges matching. Pin if necessary. Stitch diagonal, and press.

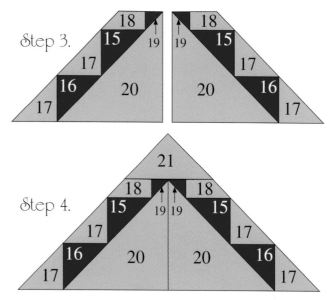

Join the two sections shown in Step 3 together. For Step 4, join Unit 21 triangle to the top as shown.

---

units 5, 1, 2, 1, 3, 1, 3, 4, 3, and 6. Match all points. For the second row, from left to right join: units 7, 1, 3, 4, 2, 1, 3, and 8. Be sure to match all points.

5. Join the two rows together, carefully matching points.

6. For the basket stand, (row 3), join units 12, 9, 11, 10, and 12 in a row. Join this row to the bottom row, carefully matching seams.

7. Center triangle, Unit 13 at the bottom of the basket. Press seam towards basket bottom. Trim off Unit 12 on both sides at a 45° angle, using Unit 13 as your guide. Join triangle Unit 14 to opposite sides of the basket as shown.

8. Join the basket top to the bottom as shown, matching Unit 16 seams to complete the basket.

Morning Star, Block 12

Block finishes to: 17" square.
Techniques used: Rectrangles, diagonal corners on Rectrangles, and triangle-squares.

MATERIALS FOR BLOCK 12

Fabric I (dark brown print)
Need 6 3/8"   3/8 yard
Fabric II (brown stripe)
Need 6 1/2"   3/8 yard
Fabric III (light green print)
Need 3 1/4"   1/4 yard
Fabric IV (dark green print)
Need 3 1/4"   1/4 yard

Block Diagram

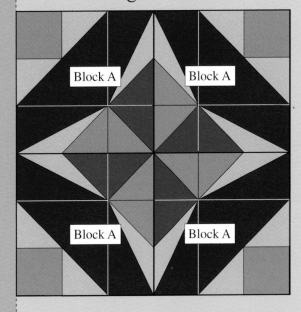

Block A   Block A

Block A   Block A

CUTTING FOR BLOCK 12

FROM FABRIC I, CUT: (DARK BROWN PRINT)
- One 6 3/8" wide strip. From this, cut:
   * Two - 6 3/8" squares (A2) cut in half diagonally.
   * Eight - 3 1/4" x 6 1/2" (A1a, A4a)

FROM FABRIC II, CUT: (BROWN STRIPE)
- One 6 1/2" strip. From this, cut:
   * Eight - 3 1/4" x 6 1/2" (A1, A4)
   * Four - 3 5/8" squares (A2b) cut in half diagonally.

FROM FABRIC III, CUT: (LIGHT GREEN PRINT)
- One 3 1/4" wide strip. From this, cut:
   * Twelve - 3 1/4" squares (A1b, A2a, A3)

FROM FABRIC IV, CUT: (DARK GREEN PRINT)
- One 3 1/4" wide strip. From this, cut:
   * Eight - 3 1/4" squares (A3, A4b)

Block A Assembly

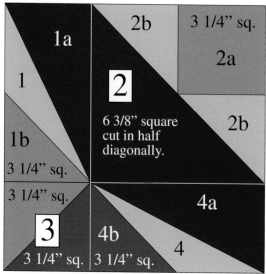

Block A. Make 4. When completed block should measure 8 3/4"square.

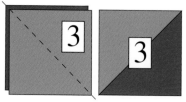

Place 3 1/4" squares of fabrics III and IV, right sides facing, and raw edges matching. Stitch diagonal, trim seam and press. Make 4.

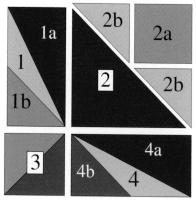

Join triangles Unit 2b to sides of Unit 2a; then place triangle Unit 2 right sides facing and raw edges matching on top of the 2a-2b combined units. Use 1/4" seam and stitch on long bias edge. Open and press. Join Unit 1 to left side of Unit 2. Join units 3 and 4; then add them to the bottom of combined 1-2 units, matching seams. Make 4 for Block A.

Making mirror image units 1 and 4

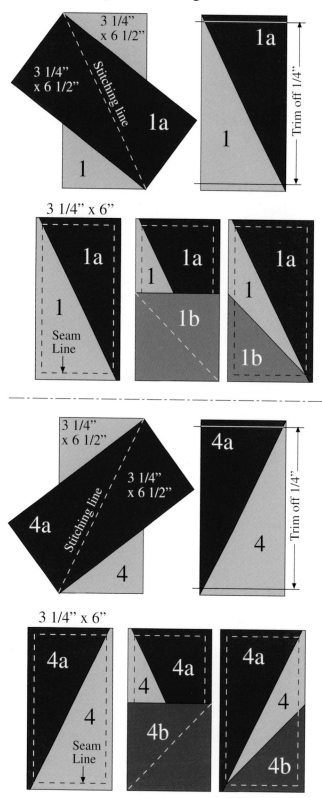

1. Refer to the diagrams above for making the Rectrangles. Complete instructions for Rectrangle units begin on page 8. Join diagonal corners to the Rectrangle units as shown. Make four each of units 1 and 4.

2. Refer to the diagram and instructions at left to piece Block A. Make 4. Join the four Block A's as shown in Block Diagram on page 42, and match seams carefully, to complete the block.

Mariner's Star, Block 13

Block finishes to: 17" square.
Techniques used: Rectrangles and Rectrangles used as diagonal corners.

MATERIALS FOR BLOCK 13

■ **Fabric I (dark brown print)**
Need 12 1/8"   1/2 yard
■ **Fabric II (medium green print)**
Need 9 1/4"   3/8 yard
■ **Fabric III (dark orange print)**
Need 4 7/8"   1/4 yard
□ **Fabric IV (gold holly print)**
Need 4 7/8"   1/4 yard
□ **Fabric V (bright yellow/gold print)**
Need 2 7/8"   1/8 yard

Block Diagram

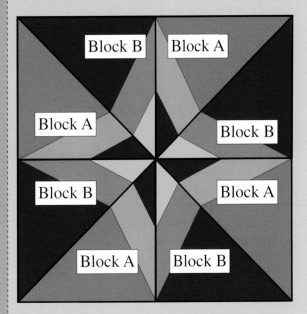

CUTTING FOR BLOCK 13

■ **FROM FABRIC I, CUT: (DARK BROWN PRINT)**
- One 9 1/4" wide strip. From this, cut:
    * Four - 9 1/4" x 9 3/4" (B2)
- One 2 7/8" wide strip. From this, cut:
    * Four - 2 7/8" x 5 3/4" (A1a)

■ **FROM FABRIC II, CUT: (MEDIUM GREEN PRINT)**
- One 9 1/4" strip. From this, cut:
    * Four - 9 1/4" x 9 3/4" (A2)

■ **FROM FABRIC III, CUT: (DARK ORANGE PRINT)**
- One 4 7/8" wide strip. From this, cut:
    * Four - 4 7/8" x 9 3/4" (B1)

□ **FROM FABRIC IV, CUT: (GOLD HOLLY PRINT)**
- One 4 7/8" wide strip. From this, cut:
    * Four - 4 7/8" x 9 3/4" (A1)

□ **FROM FABRIC V, CUT: (BRIGHT YELLOW/GOLD CHECK)**
- One 2 7/8" wide strip. From this, cut:
    * Four - 2 7/8" x 5 3/4" (B1a)

Blocks A and B Assembly

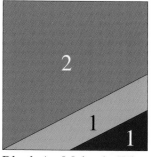

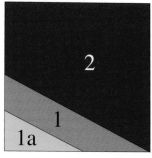

Block A. Make 4. When completed, block should measure 8 3/4" square.

Block B. Make 4. When completed, block should measure 8 3/4" square.

Making Block A

Step 1

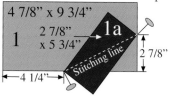

Measure up 2 7/8" on side of Unit 1 as shown. Place pins for a guide. Place the rectrangle top right corner at the 2 7/8" point. Pivot rectrangle until bottom left corner matches bottom raw edge of Unit 1. Bottom left corner should be 4 1/4" from bottom left side of Rectrangle. Pin in place, and stitch along diagonal line. Press in place as in diagram on right. When making Unit 1, if Rectrangle presses even with bottom unit, trim off bottom (base) fabric, leaving seam allowance when you trim to avoid unneccesary thickness.

Step 2

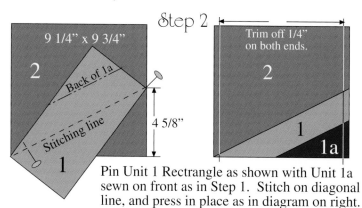

Pin Unit 1 Rectrangle as shown with Unit 1a sewn on front as in Step 1. Stitch on diagonal line, and press in place as in diagram on right. Trim off 1/4" as shown in diagram on right.

9 1/4" square.

Step 3

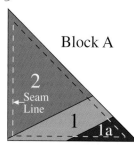

Making Block B

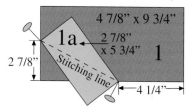

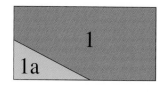

Block B is a mirror image of Block A, with different colors. Refer to instructions for Block A.

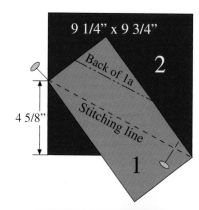

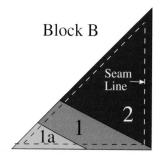

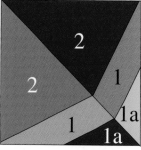

Join A and B blocks together. Carefully match seams. Make 4. Refer to Block diagram for correct position of the Blocks. Trim to 17" if necessary when block is complete.

Jig Saw Puzzle, Block 14

Block finishes to: 17" square.
Techniques used: Rectrangles,
Rectrangles used as diagonal corners,
and diagonal corners.

MATERIALS FOR BLOCK 14

■ **Fabric I (dark brown print)**
Need 5 3/4"   1/4 yard
□ **Fabric II (gold holly print)**
Need 7 7/8"   3/8 yard
▨ **Fabric III (dark orange print)**
Need 7 7/8"   3/8 yard
▨ **Fabric IV (light green print)**
Need 2 7/8"   3/8 yard
▨ **Fabric V (dark rust print)**
Need 2 7/8"   1/8 yard

Block Diagram

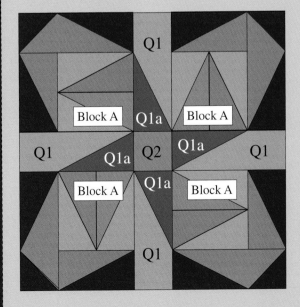

CUTTING FOR BLOCK 14

■ **FROM FABRIC I, CUT: (DARK BROWN PRINT)**
• **One 5 3/4" wide strip. From this, cut:**
   * Eight - 2 7/8" x 5 3/4" (3a, 4a)
   Stack this cut:
   * Four - 2 7/8" squares (4b)

□ **FROM FABRIC II, CUT: (GOLD HOLLY PRINT)**
• **One 7 7/8" wide strip. From this, cut:**
   * Four - 2 7/8" x 7 7/8" (Q1)
   * Eight - 2 7/8" x 5 3/4" (1, 2)

▨ **FROM FABRIC III, CUT: (DARK ORANGE PRINT)**
• **One 7 7/8" wide strip. From this, cut:**
   * Four - 2 7/8" x 7 7/8" (4)
   * Eight - 2 7/8" x 5 3/4" (2a, 3)

▨ **FROM FABRIC III, CUT: (LIGHT GREEN PRINT)**
• **One 2 7/8" wide strip. From this, cut:**
   * Four - 2 7/8" x 5 3/4" (1a)
   * One - 2 7/8" square (Q2)

▨ **FROM FABRIC V, CUT: (DARK RUST PRINT)**
• **One 2 7/8" wide strip. From this, cut:**
   * Four - 2 7/8" x 5 3/4" (Q1a)

Block A Assembly

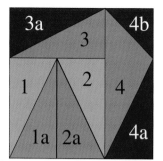

Block A. Make 4. When completed, block should measure 7 5/8" square.

1. Refer to the diagrams to make the Rectrangles. Complete instructions for Rectrangle units begin on page 8. Make four of each Rectrangle.

2. To piece Block A, join Rectrangle units 1 and 2 as shown; then add Unit 3 to the top of the combined 1-2 units. Join Unit 4 to the right side. Make 4 of Block A.

3. Refer to Block Diagram on page 46 for correct positioning of the Block and "Q" units. Join Block A to opposite sides of Unit Q1. Make 2. Join remaining Q1 units to opposite sides of Unit Q2; then join top and bottom of block to the Q1-Q2 combination, carefully matching seams to complete the block.

Making Unit 1

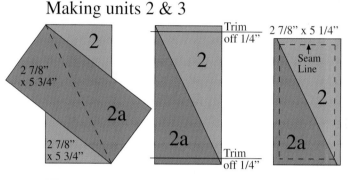

Making units 2 & 3

Unit 3 is made the same as Unit 2. Follow diagram of Unit 2 above for correct assembly, and refer to block diagram for correct color.

Making Unit Q1

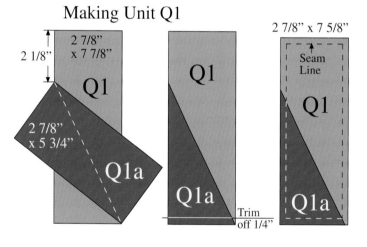

Making unit 4

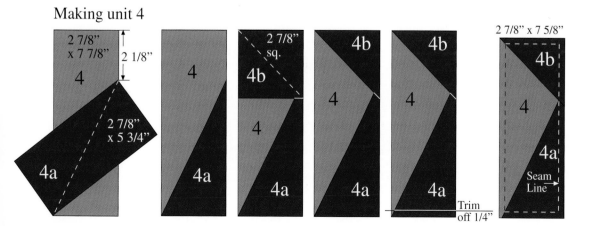

Log Cabin Flower, Block 15

Block finishes to: 17" square.
Techniques used: Rectrangles, Rectrangles used as diagonal corners, and diagonal corners.

MATERIALS FOR BLOCK 15

- **Fabric I (dark barn red check)**
  Need 3"   1/8 yard
- **Fabric II (barn red print)**
  Need 2 1/2"   1/8 yard
- **Fabric III (dark orange print)**
  Need 2 1/2"   1/8 yard
- **Fabric IV (bright yellow/gold check)**
  Need 4" square   Scrap
- **Fabric V (dark green print)**
  Need 3"   1/4 yard
- **Fabric VI (medium green print)**
  Need 3 1/2" square   Scrap
- **Fabric VII (brown stripe)**
  Need 7 3/4"   1/4 yard

CUTTING FOR BLOCK 15

- **FROM FABRIC I, CUT:**
  (DARK BARN RED CHECK)
- One 3" wide strip. From this, cut:
    * One - 3" x 13 1/2 (11)
    * One - 3" x 11" (10)

- **FROM FABRIC II, CUT:**
  (BARN RED PRINT)
- One 2 1/2" strip. From this, cut:
    * One - 2 1/2" x 9 1/4" (7)
    * One - 2 1/2" x 7 1/4" (6)

- **FROM FABRIC III, CUT:**
  (DARK ORANGE PRINT)
- One 2 1/2" wide strip. From this, cut:
    * One - 21/2" x 7" (5)
    * One - 2 1/2" x 5" (4)

- **FROM FABRIC IV, CUT:**
  (BRIGHT YELLOW/GOLD CHECK)
- One - 3 3/4" square (1)

- **FROM FABRIC V, CUT:**
  (DARK GREEN PRINT)
- One 3" wide strip. From this, cut:
    * One - 3" x 17 1/4" (15)
    * One - 3" x 14 3/4" (14)

- **FROM FABRIC VI, CUT:**
  (MEDIUM GREEN PRINT)
- One - 3" square (11b)

- **FROM FABRIC VII, CUT:**
  (BROWN STRIPE)
- One 6" wide strip. From this, cut:
    * Four - 3" x 6" (10a, 11a, 14a, 15a)
    * Two - 2 1/2" x 5" (6a, 7a)
    * One - 1 3/4" x 5" (3)
    * One - 1 3/4" x 3 3/4" (2)
    * One - 3" square (15b)
  Stack these cuts:
    * Two - 2 1/2" squares (4a, 5a)
    * One - 2 1/4" x 10 3/4" (9)
    * One - 2 1/4" x 9" (8)
    * Two 1 3/4" squares (1a)
- One 1 3/4" wide strip. From this, cut:
    * One - 1 3/4" x 14 1/2" (13)
    * One - 1 3/4" x 13 1/4" (12)

Block Diagram

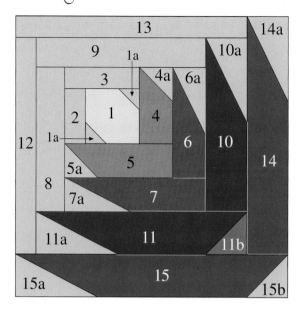

Block Assembly

Making mirror image units 6 and 7.

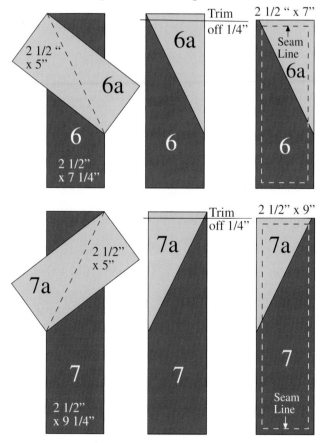

1. Refer to the diagrams to make the Rectrangles. Complete instructions for Rectrangle units begin on page 8. Make one of each Rectrangle.

2. Use diagonal corner technique to make one of units 1, 4, 5, 11, and 15.

Making units 10 and 14.

Units 10 and 14 are made the same way, the only difference is the color and length of Unit 14. Unit 14 is 3" x 14 3/4". After trimming, it is 3" x 14 1/2". Refer to the diagram below, and the Block Diagram to make both units.

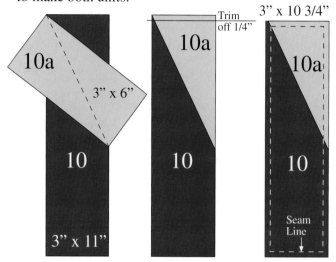

Making units 11 and 15.

Units 11 and 15 are made the same way, the only difference is the color and length of Unit 15. Unit 15 is 3" x 17 1/4". After trimming, it is 3" x 17". Unit 11b diagonal corner is Fabric VI, and Unit 15b diagonal corner is Fabric VII. Refer to the diagram below, and the Block Diagram to make both units.

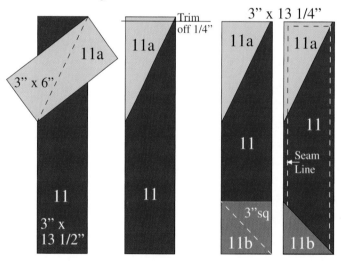

3. To piece the log cabin block, join units 1 and 2; then add Unit 3 to the top. Join Unit 4 to the right side. Join Unit 5 to the bottom; then add Unit 6 to the right side. Join Unit 7 to the bottom of the block; then join Unit 8 to the left side of the block as shown. Join Unit 9 to the top of the block. Join Unit 10 to the right side; then add Unit 11 to the bottom. Join Unit 12 to the left side of the block; then add Unit 13 to the top. Join Unit 14 to the right side; then join Unit 15 to the bottom to complete the block.

Wheel Of Fortune, Block 16

Block finishes to: 17" square.
Techniques used: Rectrangles, diagonal corners, and triangle-squares.

MATERIALS FOR BLOCK 16

Fabric I (dark brown print)
Need 6 3/8"   1/4 yard

Fabric II (brown stripe)
Need 11"   3/8 yard

Fabric III (dark gold print)
Need 6 3/8"   1/4 yard

Fabric IV (dark rust print)
Need 5 3/4"   1/4 yard

Fabric V (bright yellow/gold check)
Need 2 7/8"   1/8 yard

Fabric VI (gold holly print)
Need 2 7/8"   1/8 yard

CUTTING FOR BLOCK 16

FROM FABRIC I, CUT: (DARK BROWN PRINT)
• One 6 3/8" wide strip. From this, cut:
  * Four - 6 3/8" squares (5)

FROM FABRIC II, CUT: (BROWN STRIPE)
• One 5 3/4" wide strip. From this, cut:
  * Eight - 2 7/8" x 5 3/4" (2, 3)
• One 5 1/4" wide strip. From this, cut:
  * Four - 5 1/4" squares (5a)

FROM FABRIC III, CUT: (DARK GOLD PRINT)
• One 6 3/8" wide strip. From this, cut:
  * Four - 6 3/8" squares (5)
  * Four - 1 5/8" x 5 1/4" (4)

FROM FABRIC IV, CUT: (DARK RUST PRINT)
• One 5 3/4" wide strip. From this, cut:
  * Eight - 2 7/8" x 5 3/4" (2a, 3a)

FROM FABRIC V, CUT: (BRIGHT YELLOW/GOLD CHECK)
• One 2 7/8" wide strip. From this, cut:
  * Two - 2 7/8" x 5 1/4" (1)

FROM FABRIC VI, CUT: (GOLD HOLLY PRINT)
• One 2 7/8" wide strip. From this, cut:
  * Four - 2 7/8" squares (1a)

Block Diagram

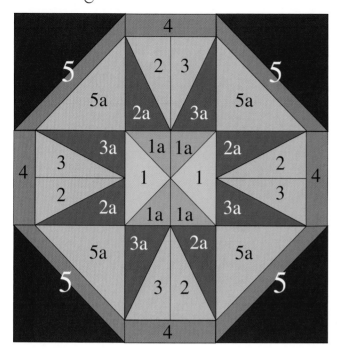

Making mirror image units 2 and 3.

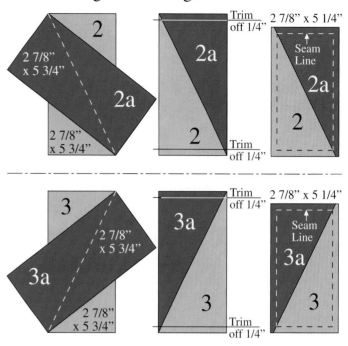

Block Assembly

Making Unit 5

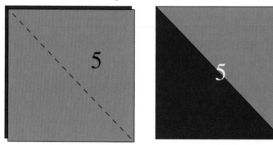

Place 6 3/8" squares of fabrics I and III right sides together with raw edges matching. Pin in place and stitch diagonally as shown. Press towards darkest fabric and trim your seam.

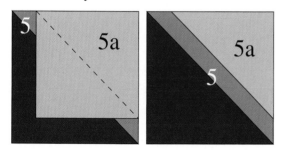

Place diagonal corner 5a as shown. Stitch diagonal, trim seam and press. Make 4.

1. Refer to the diagrams to make the Rectrangles. Complete instructions for Rectrangle units begin on page 8. Make four of each Rectrangle.
2. Use diagonal corner technique to make two of Units 1.
3. Refer to the diagram at left to make the large triangle-square with a diagonal corner added. Follow the instructions given.
4. To piece the block, join Rectrangle units 2 and 3 as shown in block diagram. Carefully match the point. Join Unit 4 to the pointed end of each 2-3 pair. Join units 1 as shown, forming the center of the block.
5. Join combined 2-4 units to top and bottom of the center section as shown. Refer to Block Diagram for correct position of Unit 5 and join Unit 5 to opposite sides of remaining combined 2-4 units as shown. Make 2 and join them to opposite sides of the center section, matching seams to complete the block.

Double Bear Paw, Block 17

Block finishes to: 17" square.
Techniques used: Rectrangles with diagonal corners.

MATERIALS FOR BLOCK 17

Fabric I (dark brown print)
Need 4 1/4"   1/4 yard
Fabric II (gold holly print)
Need 9"   3/8 yard
Fabric III (dark gold print)
Need 2"   1/8 yard
Fabric IV (light green print)
Need 2"   1/8 yard
Fabric V (dark rust print)
Need 4 3/4"   1/4 yard

CUTTING FOR BLOCK 17

FROM FABRIC I, CUT: (DARK BROWN PRINT)
- **One 4 1/4" wide strip. From this, cut:**
  * Four - 4 1/4" squares (A4)

FROM FABRIC II, CUT: (GOLD HOLLY PRINT)
- **One 4 3/4" wide strip. From this, cut:**
  * Sixteen - 2 3/8" x 4 3/4" (A1, A3)
- **One 4 1/4" wide strip. From this, cut:**
  * Four - 4 1/4" squares (A2)
  * Four - 2" x 4 1/4" - (Q3)

FROM FABRIC III, CUT: (DARK GOLD PRINT)
- **One 2" wide strip. From this, cut:**
  * Sixteen - 2" squares (A1b, A3b)

FROM FABRIC IV, CUT: (LIGHT GREEN PRINT)
- **One 2" wide strip. From this, cut:**
  * Four - 2" x 4 1/4" (Q2)

FROM FABRIC V, CUT: (DARK RUST PRINT)
- **One 4 3/4" wide strip. From this, cut:**
  * Sixteen - 2 3/8" x 4 3/4" (A1a, A3a)
  * One - 2" square (Q1)

Block Diagram

Making mirror image units 1 and 3.

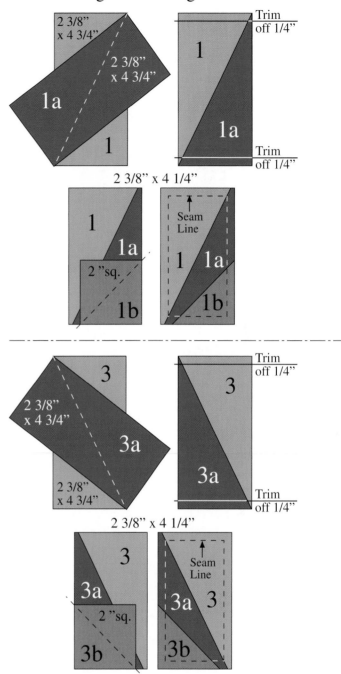

Block A Assembly

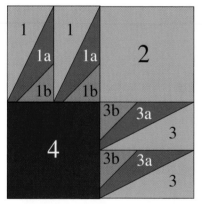

Block A. Make 4. When completed, block should measure 8" square.

1. Refer to the diagrams to make the Rectrangles with diagonal corners. Complete instructions for Rectrangle units begin on page 8. Make eight of each Rectrangle.

2. To assemble Block A, refer to the diagram above and join two of Unit 1 Rectrangles as shown, and two of Unit 3 Rectrangles. You will have four pairs of each. Join Unit 2 to right side of the Unit 1 pairs. Join Unit 4 to the left side of the Unit 3 pairs. Join the top and bottom sections of the block together, matching corner seams.

3. Join units Q2 and Q3. Make 4. Referring to Block

Diagram, join Block A to opposite sides of combined units Q2-Q3. Make 2.

4. For the center sashing, join the remaining combined Q2-Q3 units to opposite sides of Unit Q1. Join the top and bottom combined sections to top and bottom of the center sashing, matching seams carefully to complete the block.

Sampler Quilt Border, Block 18

Block finishes to: 17" square.
Techniques used: Rectrangles.

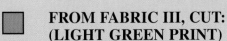

MATERIALS FOR BORDER BLOCK 18

■ **Fabric I (dark brown print)**
Need 15 1/8"   1/2 yard

□ **Fabric II (leafy tan print)**
Need 16 3/4"   5/8 yard

■ **Fabric III (light green print)**
Need 24"   7/8 yard

■ **Fabric IV (dark green print)**
Need 11 1/4"   1/2 yard

■ **Fabric V (dark rust print)**
Need 24"   7/8 yard

■ **Fabric VI (dark gold print)**
Need 12"   1/2 yard

■ **Fabric VII (gold holly print)**
Need 10"   3/8 yard

CUTTING FOR BLOCK 18

■ **FROM FABRIC 1, CUT: (DARK BROWN PRINT)**
- **Three 3 7/8" wide strips. From these, cut:**
  * Twenty-one - 3 7/8" squares (10) cut in half diagonally
  * Ten - 3 1/2" squares (4)
- **One 3 1/2" wide strip. From this, cut:**
  * Four - 3 1/2" squares (add to 4)

□ **FROM FABRIC II, CUT: (LEAFY TAN PRINT)**
- **One 9 1/4" wide strip. From this, cut:**
  * Fourteen - 1 1/4" x 9 1/4" (13)
  * Fourteen - 1 1/4" x 8 3/4" (7)
  * Four - 1 1/4" x 7 3/4" (11)
- **Six 1 1/4" wide strips. From these, cut:**
  * Ten - 1 1/4" x 7 3/4" (add to 11)
  * Fourteen - 1 1/4" x 6 1/2" (6)

■ **FROM FABRIC III, CUT: (LIGHT GREEN PRINT)**
- **Six 4" wide strips. From these, cut:**
  * 112 - 2" x 4" (1, 3)

■ **FROM FABRIC IV, CUT: (DARK GREEN PRINT)**
- **Two 3 7/8" wide strips. From these, cut:**
  * Fourteen - 3 7/8" squares (9) cut in half diagonally
  * Seven - 3 1/2" squares (2)
- **One 3 1/2" wide strip. From this, cut:**
  * Seven - 3 1/2" sq. (add to 2)

■ **FROM FABRIC V, CUT: (RUST TEXTURED PRINT)**
- **Six 4" wide strips. From these, cut:**
  * 112 - 2" x 4" (1a, 3a)

■ **FROM FABRIC VI, CUT: (DARK GOLD PRINT)**
- **Six 2" wide strips. From these, cut:**
  * Twenty-eight - 2" x 7 1/4" (8, 14)

■ **FROM FABRIC VII, CUT: (GOLD HOLLY PRINT)**
- **Five 2" wide strips. From these, cut:**
  * Twenty-eight - 2" x 6 1/2" (5, 12)

Block Diagram

Border Block 18. Make 14. When completed, block should measure 17" long on the straight.

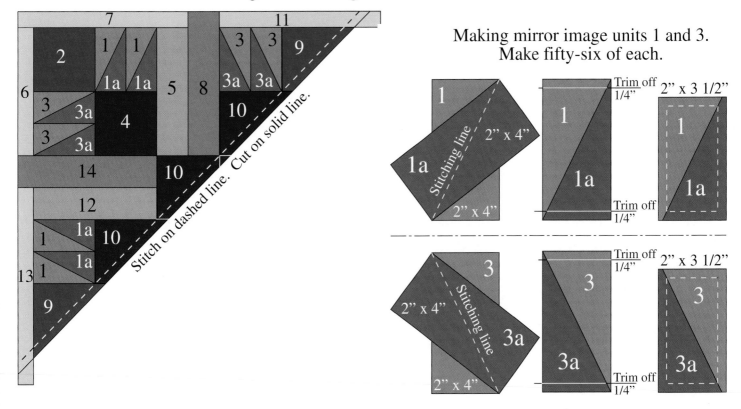

Making mirror image units 1 and 3.
Make fifty-six of each.

Block Assembly

1. Refer to the diagrams to make the Rectrangles. Complete instructions for Rectrangle units begin on page 8. Make fifty-six of each Rectrangle.

2. To assemble the block, refer to the diagram above and join two of Unit 1 Rectrangles as shown, and two of Unit 3 Rectrangles. You will make twenty-eight pairs of each. For the top left portion of the block, join Unit 2 to the left side of the fourteen pairs of joined units 1. Join Unit 4 to the right side of the fourteen pairs of joined units 3. Join the top and bottom of this section together, matching corner seams. Join Unit 5 to the right side of this section; then add Unit 6 to the left side. Join Unit 7 on the top as shown.

3. Join Unit 8 to the right side of the corner section. Join the remaining fourteen pairs of Unit 3 to the top of triangle, Unit 10; then add triangle, Unit 9 to the right side. Join Unit 11 to the top of these combined units. Do not trim Unit 11 at this time. Join this section to the right side of the corner section, trimming off the tip of triangle, Unit 10 even with the bottom raw edge.

4. For the bottom section of the block, join fourteen remaining Unit 1's to left side of triangle, Unit 10; then add triangle, Unit 9 to the bottom. Join Unit 12 to the top as shown; then add Unit 13 to the left side. Join Unit 14 to the top of this section; then add the final Unit 10 triangle to the right side of combined units 12-14.

5. Join this section to the bottom of the block as shown, matching corner seams.

6. The dashed line is your seam line. Lay a ruler across the bias raw edge of the triangle block, and using the triangles as a guide, trim off units 11 and 13 to complete the block. Make 14.

 Sampler Quilt

Quilt finishes to: 84 1/4" x 110 1/2".
Techniques used for sashing: triangle-squares.

MATERIALS FOR SASHING AND BINDING.

Fabric I (dark rust print)
Need 73 3/8"   2 1/4 yards
Fabric II (honey tan batik)
Need 45 7/8""   1 3/8 yards
Backing   7 1/2 yards

CUTTING FOR SASHING AND BINDING.

FROM FABRIC I, CUT: (DARK RUST PRINT)
- **One 3 7/8" wide strip. From this, cut:**
    * One - 3 7/8" square (Q9) cut in half diagonally
    * Two - 3 1/2" x 17" (Q7)
- **Twelve 3 1/2" wide strips. From these, cut:**
    * Three - 3 1/2" x 20" (Q2, Q8) Trim to fit.
    * Four - 3 1/2" x 19" (Q1) Trim to fit.
    * Fifteen - 3 1/2" x 17" (add to Q7 above)
    * Eighteen - 3 1/2" squares (For Q3 triangle-squares)
- **Eleven 2 1/2" wide strips for straight-grain binding.**

FROM FABRIC II, CUT: (HONEY TAN BATIK)
- **One 3 7/8" wide strip. From this, cut:**
    * One - 3 7/8" square (Q10) cut in half diagonally
    * Two - 3 1/2" x 17" (Q5)
- **Twelve 3 1/2" wide strips. From these, cut:**
    * Five - 3 1/2" x 20" (Q4, Q6)
    * Seventeen - 3 1/2" x 17" (add to Q5 above)
    * Eighteen - 3 1/2" squares (Q3 triangle-squares)

Making The Triangle-squares.

Make 18

Place 3 1/2" squares of fabrics I and II right sides facing and raw edges matching. Stitch diagonal, trim seam and press.

57

Quilt Assembly.

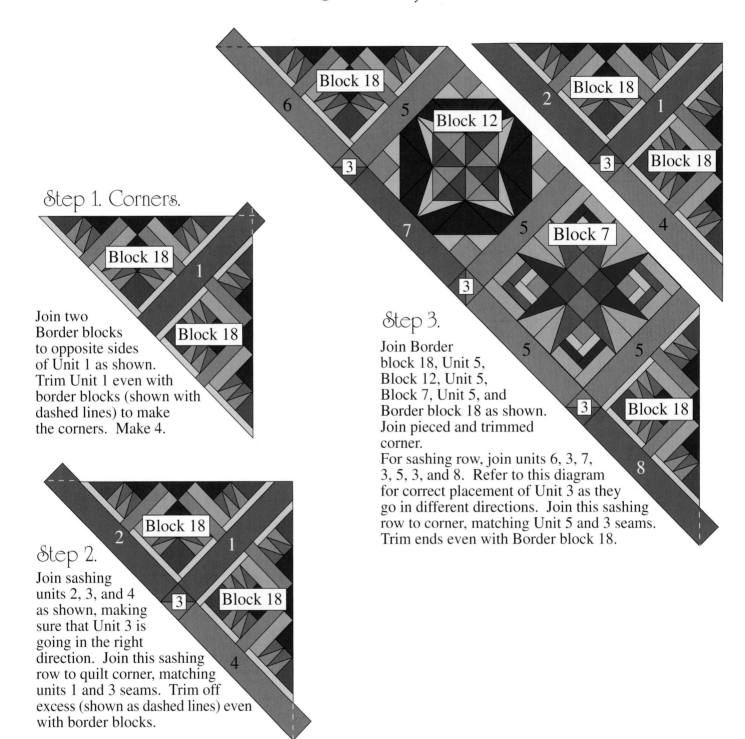

Step 1. Corners.

Join two
Border blocks
to opposite sides
of Unit 1 as shown.
Trim Unit 1 even with
border blocks (shown with
dashed lines) to make
the corners. Make 4.

Step 2.

Join sashing
units 2, 3, and 4
as shown, making
sure that Unit 3 is
going in the right
direction. Join this sashing
row to quilt corner, matching
units 1 and 3 seams. Trim off
excess (shown as dashed lines) even
with border blocks.

Step 3.

Join Border
block 18, Unit 5,
Block 12, Unit 5,
Block 7, Unit 5, and
Border block 18 as shown.
Join pieced and trimmed
corner.
For sashing row, join units 6, 3, 7,
3, 5, 3, and 8. Refer to this diagram
for correct placement of Unit 3 as they
go in different directions. Join this sashing
row to corner, matching Unit 5 and 3 seams.
Trim ends even with Border block 18.

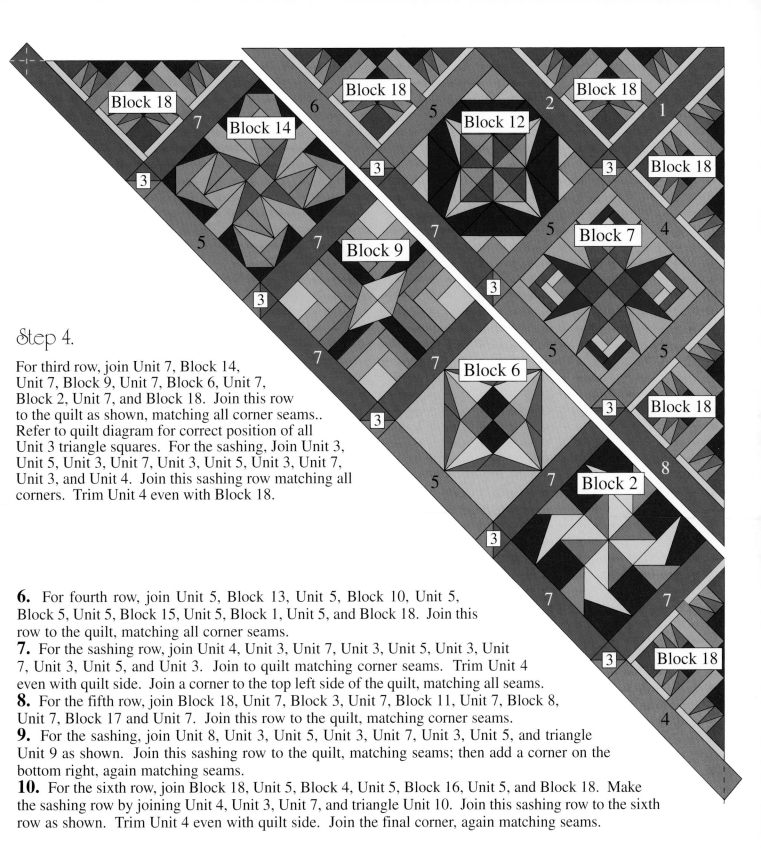

Step 4.

For third row, join Unit 7, Block 14,
Unit 7, Block 9, Unit 7, Block 6, Unit 7,
Block 2, Unit 7, and Block 18. Join this row
to the quilt as shown, matching all corner seams..
Refer to quilt diagram for correct position of all
Unit 3 triangle squares. For the sashing, Join Unit 3,
Unit 5, Unit 3, Unit 7, Unit 3, Unit 5, Unit 3, Unit 7,
Unit 3, and Unit 4. Join this sashing row matching all
corners. Trim Unit 4 even with Block 18.

6. For fourth row, join Unit 5, Block 13, Unit 5, Block 10, Unit 5,
Block 5, Unit 5, Block 15, Unit 5, Block 1, Unit 5, and Block 18. Join this
row to the quilt, matching all corner seams.
7. For the sashing row, join Unit 4, Unit 3, Unit 7, Unit 3, Unit 5, Unit 3, Unit
7, Unit 3, Unit 5, and Unit 3. Join to quilt matching corner seams. Trim Unit 4
even with quilt side. Join a corner to the top left side of the quilt, matching all seams.
8. For the fifth row, join Block 18, Unit 7, Block 3, Unit 7, Block 11, Unit 7, Block 8,
Unit 7, Block 17 and Unit 7. Join this row to the quilt, matching corner seams.
9. For the sashing, join Unit 8, Unit 3, Unit 5, Unit 3, Unit 7, Unit 3, Unit 5, and triangle
Unit 9 as shown. Join this sashing row to the quilt, matching seams; then add a corner on the
bottom right, again matching seams.
10. For the sixth row, join Block 18, Unit 5, Block 4, Unit 5, Block 16, Unit 5, and Block 18. Make
the sashing row by joining Unit 4, Unit 3, Unit 7, and triangle Unit 10. Join this sashing row to the sixth
row as shown. Trim Unit 4 even with quilt side. Join the final corner, again matching seams.

Quilting And Finishing.

Mary ditched the patchwork, and worked a small stipple in open areas. The sashing was quilted with a beautiful feather motif. Make 440" of straight-grain binding from Fabric I, and bind your quilt. See page 13 for binding.

Checkerboard Prairie Stars Queen

Whether in a victorian or contemporary setting, this quilt fits in any-where. There is a very subtle change in the checkerboard fabrics that we used; one a print, and one a solid of the same tones. One simple Rectrangle is used, making it a breeze to complete. Perfect for a beginner. Mix and match your fabrics, and enjoy the final outcome!

Quilt finishes to: 87" x 107 1/2"
Techniques used: Rectrangles, diago-nal corners and triangle-squares.

MATERIALS FOR QUILT

Fabric I (light peach solid)
Need 129"   3 3/4 yards

Fabric II (medium peach print)
Need 129"   3 3/4 yards

Fabric III (dark peach floral print)
Need 22 1/2"   3/4 yard

Fabric IV (light green dotted print)
Need 75"   2 1/4 yards

Fabric V (dark green solid)
Need 110 1/2"   3 1/4 yards
Backing   7 7/8 yards

CUTTING FOR QUILT

FROM FABRIC I, CUT: (LIGHT PEACH SOLID

- **Three 9 1/2" wide strips. From these, cut:**
    * Forty - 2 1/2" x 9 1/2" (A10, B15, C15, E6)
    Stack this cut:
    * Seventy-eight - 1 1/2" squares (A7a, B11a, B13a, C11a, C13a, E4a)
- **Three 7 1/2" wide strips. From these, cut:**
    * Forty - 2 1/2" x 7 1/2" (A8, B12, C12, E5)
    Stack this cut:
    * Sixty-five - 1 1/2" squares (add to 1 1/2" sq)

- **Seven 6 1/2" wide strips. From these, cut:**
    * Forty - 6 1/2" squares (A6, B6, C6, E3)
    Stack this cut:
    * Seventeen - 1 1/2" squares (add to 1 1/2" sq.)
- **Five 5" wide strips. From these, cut:**
    * Eighty - 2 1/2" x 5" (A4a, B4a, C4a, E2a)
- **Three 2 1/2" wide strips. From these, cut:**
    * Forty-eight - 2 1/2" squares (B1a, B2a, B7, C1a, C2a, C7, D1)

FROM FABRIC II, CUT: (MED. PEACH PRINT)

- **Three 9 1/2" wide strips. From these, cut:**
  - * Forty - 2 1/2" x 9 1/2" (A11, B14, C14, D6)
  - Stack this cut:
  - * Seventy-eight - 1 1/2" squares (A7b, B9a, B13b, C9a, C13b, D4a)
- **Three 7 1/2" wide strips. From these, cut:**
  - * Forty - 2 1/2" x 7 1/2" (A9, B10, C10, D5)
  - Stack this cut:
  - * Sixty-five - 1 1/2" squares (add to 1 1/2" sq)
- **Seven 6 1/2" wide strips. From these, cut:**
  - * Forty - 6 1/2" squares (A5, B5, C5, D3)
  - Stack this cut:
  - * Seventeen - 1 1/2" squares (add to 1 1/2" sq.)
- **Five 5" wide strips. From these, cut:**
  - * Eighty - 2 1/2" x 5" (A3a, B3a, C3a, D2a)
- **Three 2 1/2" wide strips. From these, cut:**
  - * Forty-eight - 2 1/2" squares (B1b, B2b, B8, C1b, C2b, E1)

FROM FABRIC III, CUT: (DK. PEACH FLORAL PRINT)

- **Nine 2 1/2" wide strips. Seven for straight-grain binding. From remainder, cut:**
  - * 144 - 2 1/2" squares (A1a, A2a)

FROM FABRIC IV, CUT: (LIGHT GREEN DOTTED PRINT)

- **Six 5" wide strips. From these, cut:**
  - * Ninety-six - 2 1/2" x 5" (A3, A4)
- **Three 4 1/2" strips. From these, cut:**
  - * Forty-eight - 2 1/2" x 4 1/2" (A2)
- **Three 2 1/2" wide strips. From these, cut:**
  - * Forty-eight - 2 1/2" squares (A5a, A6a)
- **Twelve 2" wide strips. From these, cut:**
  - * Four - 2" x 40" (Q3, Q4)
  - * Four - 2" x 32 3/4" (Q3) Piece two to opposite ends of two 2" x 40" strips to = two 104 1/2" lengths.
  - * Four - 2" x 24 1/4" (Q4) Piece two to opposite ends of two 2" x 40" strips to = two 87 1/2" lengths.

FROM FABRIC V, CUT: (DARK GREEN SOLID)

- **Four 5" wide strips. From these, cut:**
  - * Sixty-four - 2 1/2" x 5" (B3, B4, C3, C4, D2, E2)
- **Four 4 1/2" wide strips. From these, cut:**
  - * Twelve - 4 1/2" squares (A1)
  - * Twenty-eight - 2 1/2" x 4 1/2" (B1, B2, C1, C2)
  - Stack this cut:

- * Thirty-six - 1 1/2" x 2 1/2" (B9, B11, C9, C11, D4, E4)
- **Twenty-nine 2 1/2" wide strips. Ten for straight-grain binding. From remainder, cut:**
  - * Four - 2 1/2" x 40" (Q1, Q2)
  - * Four - 2 1/2" x 30 3/4" (Q1) Piece two to opposite ends of two 2" x 40" strips to = two 100 1/2" lengths.
  - * Four - 2 1/2" x 22 3/4" (Q2) Piece two to opposite ends of two 2" x 40" strips to = two 84 1/2" lengths.
  - * 134 - 2 1/2" squares (A7, B5a, B6a, B7, B8, B13, C5a, C6a, C7, C8, C13, D1, D3a, E1, E3a)

Rectrangles For Blocks A, B, C, & D.

1. For the Rectrangles on pages 63 and 64, draw a line diagonally from one corner to the other. Place rectrangles as shown in diagrams at right. Pin if necessary so that the Rectrangles do not slip.

2. Press the top Rectrangle over as shown. Trim top Rectrangles even with foundation unit if necessary. Trim 1/4" off at the top and bottom of each unit as shown.

3. The diagrams show how the Rectrangle should look at top and bottom when 1/4" is trimmed off. The dashed lines on the third diagrams show your seam allowance, and the measurement at the top gives you the size after trimming off the top and bottom. Make the required number of each Rectrangle shown. For more on making Rectrangles, refer to page 8.

Making Unit A3 right slant. Make 24.

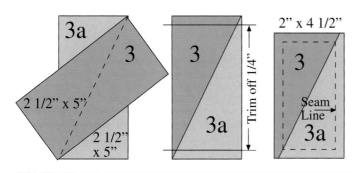

Making Unit A4 right slant. Make 24.

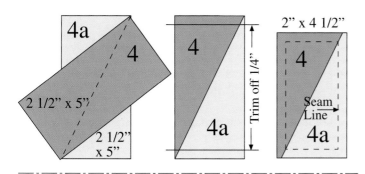

Making units B3 and C3, right slant. Make 6 for Unit B3, and 8 for Unit C3.

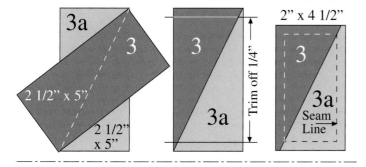

Making units B4 and C4, right slant. Make 6 For Unit B4, and 8 for Unit C4.

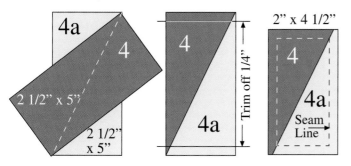

Making Units D2, right slant. Make 2.

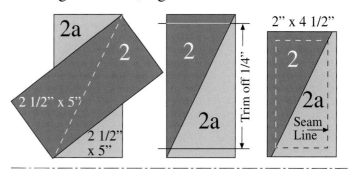

Making Unit E2 right slant. Make 2.

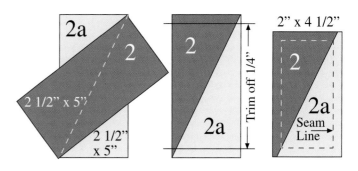

Making Unit A3 left slant. Make 24.

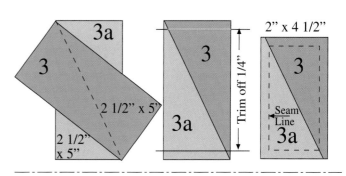

Making Unit A4 left slant. Make 24.

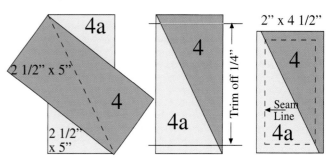

Making units B3 and C3, left slant. Make 6 for Unit B3, and 8 for Unit C3.

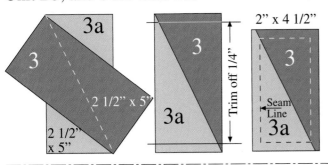

Making units B4 and C4, left slant. Make 6 for Unit B4, and 8 for Unit C4.

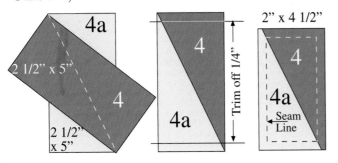

Making units D2, left slant. Make 2.

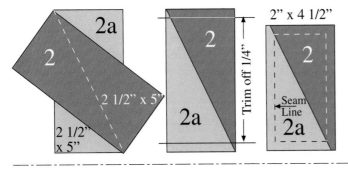

Making Unit E2 left slant. Make 2.

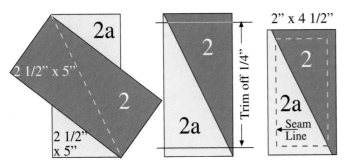

Triangle-squares.

Place 2 1/2" squares of fabrics II and V right sides facing and raw edges matching. Stitch diagonal, trim seam and press. Make 14.

Place 2 1/2" squares of fabrics II and V right sides facing and raw edges matching. Stitch diagonal, trim seam and press. Make 14.

Place 2 1/2" squares of fabrics I and V right sides facing and raw edges matching. Stitch diagonal, trim seam and press. Make 6.

Place 2 1/2" squares of fabrics I and V right sides facing and raw edges matching. Stitch diagonal, trim seam and press. Make 6.

Block A Assembly

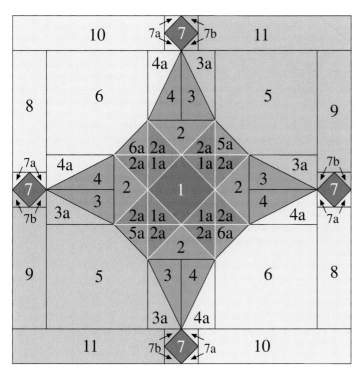

Block A. Make 12. When completed, block should measure 20 1/2" square.

1. There are four blocks in this quilt. Block A is for the quilt top, mirror image B and C blocks are for the border sides, and D and E blocks for the corners. The diagrams on pages 63 and 64 show the Rectrangles to be made for each block. The instructions tell you how many to make for each block, and the correct slant of the Rectrangle to be made. Follow the diagrams and instructions to complete the Rectrangles. Refer to page 8 for making the Rectrangles.

2. These instructions are for one block. Refer to Block A diagram and use diagonal corner technique to make four each of units 2, and 7, two each of units 5 and 6, and one of Unit 1.

3. To assemble the block, join units 3 and 4 as shown. Refer to the diagram for correct position, as they are mirror images. Join Unit 2 to the bottom of each combined 3-4 unit pairs. Working from top to bottom, join units 6, combined units 2-4, and Unit 5, carefully matching seams. Make two of these rows. One for the top, and one for the bottom row.

4. For the center row, join the remaining 2-4 combined unit pairs to opposite sides of Unit 1, matching seams. Join the three rows together as shown, again, carefully matching seams.

5. For the sides of the block, join units 8, 7, and 9 in a row. Make two rows, and join them to opposite sides of the block, carefully matching the star point seams. For the top and bottom rows, join units 10, 7,

and 11 as shown. Make two and join them to the top and bottom of the block, referring to block diagram for correct placement, and again matching seams.

B And C Block Assembly

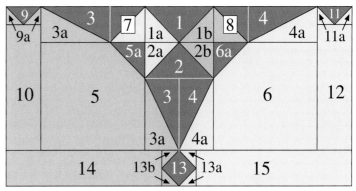

Block B. Make 6. When completed, block should measure 10 1/2" x 20 1/2".

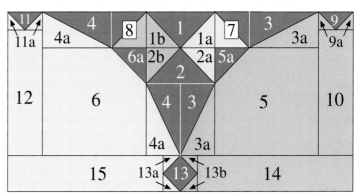

Block C. Make 8. When completed, block should measure 10 1/2" x 20 1/2".

1. These instructions are for one of each block. Refer to block diagrams above, and use diagonal corner technique to make two each of units 1, 2, 9, 11, and 13.

2. Refer to the diagrams on page 64 for making the triangle squares for blocks B, C, D, and E. Rectrangle units have been made for all blocks as directed on pages 63 and 64.

3. To assemble the blocks, join units 3 and 4 as shown. Refer to the diagrams for correct position, as they are mirror images. Join Unit 2 to the top of each combined 3-4 unit pair. Referring to block diagrams for correct placement, join Unit 5 to one side, and Unit 6 to the other, carefully matching seams.

4. Join units 3, 7, 1, 8, and 4 in a row, keeping in mind that this row is mirror imaged in Block C. Join this row to combined units 2-6 as shown, matching seams.

5. For the sides of the blocks, join units 11, and 12.

Join units 9 and 10. Join to opposite sides of the blocks, again referring to block diagrams for correct placement of mirror image units.

6. Join units 14, 13, and 15 in a row. Refer to Block C diagram for mirror image placement. Join this row to the bottom of the blocks, matching point seams to complete the blocks. Make 6 of Block B, and 8 of Block C.

D And E Block Assembly

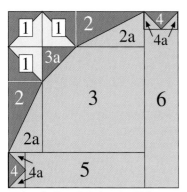

Block D. Make 2. When completed, block should measure 10 1/2"square".

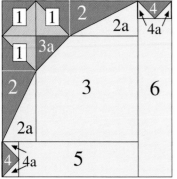

Block E. Make 2. When completed, block should measure 10 1/2"square".

1. These instructions are for one of each block. Refer to block diagrams at left, and use diagonal corner technique to make two each of Unit 4, and one of Unit 3 for each block.

2. Refer to the diagrams on page 64 for making the triangle squares for blocks B, C, D, and E. Rectrangle units have been made for all blocks as directed on pages 63 and 64.

3. To assemble the blocks, join units 1 and 2; then add Unit 3 to the right side of the 1-2 combination, matching Unit 3a seam. Refer to the block diagrams for correct placement, and join two Unit 1's together; then join Unit 2 to right side as shown. Add this row to the top of the 1-3 combined units, carefully matching seams.

4. Join units 4 and 5; then add these combined units to the bottom of the block. Join units 4 and 6. Join these combined units to the right side of the blocks to complete them. Make 2 of each block.

Quilt Assembly

1. To assemble the quilt top, join three of Block A together in a horizontal row, matching seams. Make four of these rows, and join them together as shown.

2. For side borders, refer to the quilt diagram, and join four of Block C together in a row as shown. Make two of these rows. Join the border rows to opposite sides of the quilt top, carefully matching seams.

3. For the top and bottom borders, join Block E, three Block B's, and Block D in a horizontal row as shown. Make 2. Join to the top and bottom of the quilt top, carefully matching all seams. For the borders, join previously pieced Unit Q1 to opposite sides of the quilt top. Join Unit Q2 to the top and bottom. For outer border, join previously pieced Unit Q3 to opposite sides of the quilt; then join Unit Q4 to the top and bottom to complete the quilt top.

4. Mary did wonderful things with this quilt. Note the feathered hearts in the circles in the photo on page 61. She also "ditched" the patchwork.

5. Make 400" of straight-grain binding from Fabric V, and bind your quilt. See page 13 for binding.

Quilt Assembly Diagram

Prairie Stars

When we received this throw from Mary, after she had quilted it, we all stood around it and said "Oh My!" It is probably one of my favorite pieces, and Chris' photo on page 1 gives it a personality of its own.

We liked it so well, that we added a king size quilt and pillow. Mary put the throw in her washer using "Quilting Soap", and after it line dried, the drape was awesome!

If I were a beginner, this would be my choice!

Throw finishes to: 65" square.

King/queen quilt finishes to: 100 1/2" x 111 1/2"

Techniques used: Rectrangles, triangle-squares, and diagonal corners.

MATERIALS FOR THROW

Fabric I (ivory with grape print)
Need 131"   3 7/8 yards

Fabric II (medium grape print)
Need 39"   1 1/4 yards

Fabric III (dark grape textured print)
Need 51"   1 5/8 yards

Backing   4 yards

* Thirty-two - 2 1/2" x 4 1/2" (A2)
- **Four 2 1/2" wide strips. From these, cut:**
  * Eight - 2 1/2" x 5" (add to A3, A4)
  * Four - 2 1/2" x 4 1/2" (add to A2)
  * Thirty-six - 2 1/2" squares (A5a)

FROM FABRIC III, CUT: (DK. GRAPE TEXTURED PRINT)
- **Two 8" wide strips. From these, cut:**
  * Sixteen - 2 3/4" x 8" (Q3)
  * Six - 2 3/4" x 6 3/4" (Q2)
- **One 4 1/2 wide strip. From this, cut:**
  * Nine - 4 1/2" squares (A1)
- **One 2 3/4" wide strip. From this, cut:**
  * Two - 2 3/4" x 6 3/4" (add to Q2)
  * Four - 2 3/4" squares (Q4)
  * Six - 2 1/2" squares (A6)
- **Nine 2 1/2" wide strips. Seven for straight-grain binding. From remainder, cut:**
  * Thirty - 2 1/2" squares (add to A6)
- **Three 1 3/4" wide strips. From these, cut:**
  * Fifty-six - 1 3/4" squares (Q1a)

CUTTING FOR THROW

FROM FABRIC I, CUT: (IVORY WITH GRAPE PRINT)
- **Two 9 1/2" wide strips. From these, cut:**
  * Thirty-two - 2 1/2" x 9 1/2" (A8)
- **Two 7 1/2" wide strips. From these, cut:**
  * Thirty-two - 2 1/2" x 7 1/2" (A7)
- **Six 6 1/2" wide strips. From these, cut:**
  * Thirty-six - 6 1/2" squares (A5)
  Stack this cut:
  * Seventy-two - 1 1/2" squares (A6a)
- **Four 5" wide strips. From these, cut:**
  * Sixty-four - 2 1/2" x 5" (A3a, A4a)
  * Eight - 2 1/2" squares (A1a, A2a)
- **Nine 2 1/2" wide strips. From these, cut:**
  * Four - 2 1/2" x 9 1/2" (add to A8)
  * Four - 2 1/2" x 7 1/2" (add to A7)
  * Eight - 2 1/2" x 5" (add to A3a, A4a)
  * 100 - 2 1/2" squares (add to A1a, A2a)
- **Four 2 3/4" wide strips. From these, cut:**
  * Fifty-six - 1 3/4" x 2 3/4" (Q1)
  * Fifteen - 1 1/2" squares (add to A6a)
- **Three 1 1/2" wide strips. From these, cut:**
  * Fifty-seven - 1 1/2" squares (add to A6a)

FROM FABRIC II, CUT: (MED. GRAPE PRINT)
- **Four 5" wide strips. From these, cut:**
  * Sixty-four - 2 1/2" x 5" (A3, A4)
- **Two 4 1/2" wide strips. From these, cut:**

Block A Assembly

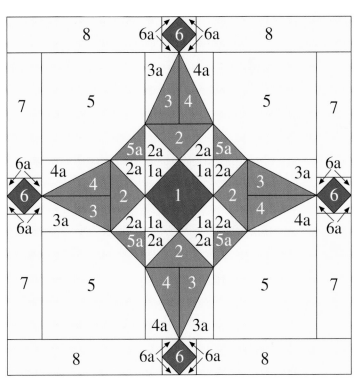

Block A. Make 9 for Throw. Make 20 for queen size quilt. When completed, block should measure 20 1/2" square.

Making units 3 and 4 for Block A. Make 36 of each for throw. Make 80 of each for quilt.

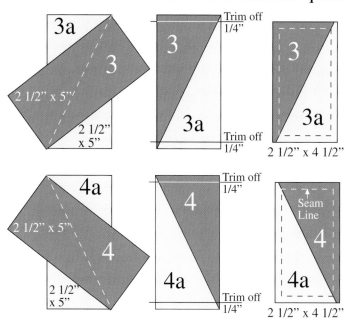

Block A Assembly

1. There is one block in this quilt. The diagrams above show the Rectrangles to be made for the block. The instructions tell you how many units to make. Follow the diagrams and instructions to complete the Rectrangles. Refer to page 8 for making the Rectrangles.

2. These instructions are for one block: Refer to Block A diagram and use diagonal corner technique to make four each of units 2, 5, and 6, and one of Unit 1. The throw has only Rectrangles and diagonal corners.

3. To assemble the block, join all units 3 and 4 as shown. Refer to the block diagram for correct position of the units. Join Unit 2 to the bottom of each combined 3-4 units pair. Working from top to bottom, for the top row, join Unit 5, combined units 2-4, and Unit 5, carefully matching seams. Make two of these rows. One for the top, and one for the bottom row.

3. For the center row, join the remaining 2-4 combined units to opposite sides of Unit 1, matching seams. Join the three rows together as shown, again, carefully matching seams.

4. For the sides of the block, join units 7, 6, and 7 in a row. Make two rows, and join them to opposite sides of the block, carefully matching the star point seams. For the top and bottom rows, join units 8, 6, and 8 as shown. Make two and join them to the top and bottom of the block, again matching seams.

Throw Assembly

Make 28

1. Join three Block A's together in a horizontal row as shown on page 71, matching star point seams. Make three rows and join the rows, again carefully matching the star point and corner seams.

2. For the border, refer to the diagram on the left, and use diagonal corner technique to make fifty-six of Unit Q1. Keep in mind that 28 are mirror images.

3. Refer to the throw diagram on page 71. Join the mirror image, Q1 units into pairs as shown above. These pairs will now be referred to as Unit Q1. Beginning with the top and bottom borders, join units Q1, Q2, Q1, Q3, Q1, Q3, Q1, Q3, Q1, Q3, Q1, Q2, and Q1 in a horizontal row. Make four. Join one to the top and one to the bottom of the throw, matching the Q1 seams to the star points and block corners.

4. For the side borders, add Unit Q4 to opposite ends of the two remaining rows; then join these rows to opposite sides of the throw, again matching seams.

Prairie Star Throw Assembly Diagram

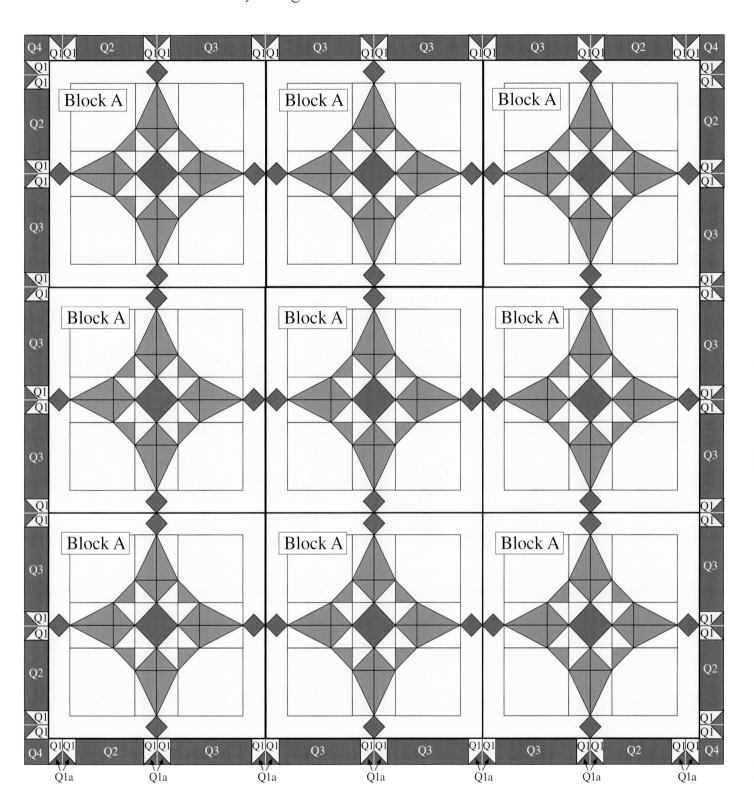

Quilting And Finishing

1. Mary quilted gorgeous feathers in the circles, and quilted larger feathers on the outer edges.
2. Make 280" of straight-grain binding, and bind the throw.   Refer to page 13 for making the binding.

MATERIALS FOR PILLOW

▢ **Fabric I (ivory with grape print)**
Need 7 1/2"   3/8 yard
▨ **Fabric II (medium grape print)**
Need 27"   7/8 yard
▩ **Fabric III (dark grape textured print)**
Need 28"   7/8 yard

Prairie Star Pillow

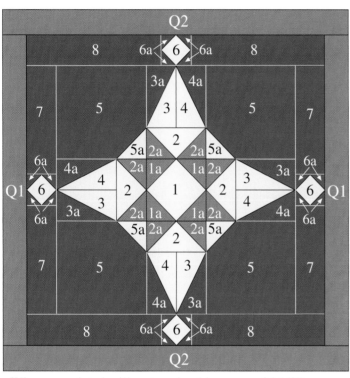

When completed, pillow top should measure 24 1/2" square.

CUTTING FOR PILLOW

▢ **FROM FABRIC I, CUT: (IVORY WITH GRAPE PRINT)**
• **One 5" wide strip. From this, cut:**
  * Eight - 2 1/2" x 5" (A3, A4)
  * One - 4 1/2" square (A1)
  * Four - 2 1/2" x 4 1/2" (A2)
• **One 2 1/2" wide strip. From this, cut:**
  * Eight - 2 1/2" squares (A5a, A6)

▨ **FROM FABRIC II, CUT: (MED. GRAPE PRINT)**
• **One 24 1/2" wide strip. From this, cut:**
  * Two - 15 1/2" x 24 1/2" (pillow backing)
  * Two - 2 1/2" x 20 1/2" (Q1)
  * Two - 2 1/2" x 24 1/2" (Q2)

• **One 2 1/2" wide strip. From this, cut:**
  * Twelve - 2 1/2" squares (A1a, A2a)
▩ **FROM FABRIC III, CUT: (DK. GRAPE TEXTURED PRINT)**
• **One 14" wide strip. From this, cut:**
  * Two - 14" x 20 1/2" (pillow backing)
• **One 6 1/2" wide strip. From this, cut:**
  * Four - 6 1/2" squares (A5)
  * Sixteen - 1 1/2" squares (A6a)
• **Three 2 1/2" wide strips. From these, cut:**
  * Eight- 2 1/2" x 5" (A3a, A4a)
  * Four - 2 1/2" x 9 1/2" (A8)
  * Four - 2 1/2" x 7 1/2" (A7)

Pillow Assembly

1. The pillow top is made the same as Block A for the throw, only the colors are different. Refer to the instructions for Block A on page 70.
2. For the borders, and backing join Unit Q1 to opposite sides of the pillow top; then join Unit Q2 to the top and bottom.
Refer to page 12 for making a flange pillow. When completed, stuff with a 20" pillow form.

MATERIALS FOR KING/QUEEN QUILT

☐ **Fabric I (ivory with grape print)**
  Need 328"   9 3/8 yards
▨ **Fabric II (medium grape print)**
  Need 100"   3 yards
■ **Fabric III (dark grape textured print)**
  Need 147 1/2"   4 1/4 yards
  Backing   8 1/4 yards

CUTTING FOR KING/QUEEN QUILT

☐ **FROM FABRIC I, CUT: (IVORY WITH GRAPE PRINT)**
- **Five 9 1/2" wide strips. From these, cut:**
  * Eighty - 2 1/2" x 9 1/2" (A8)
- **Five 7 1/2" wide strips. From these, cut:**
  * Eighty - 2 1/2" x 7 1/2" (A7)
- **Fourteen 6 1/2" wide strips. From these, cut:**
  * Eighty - 6 1/2" squares (A5)
  Stack this cut:
  * Seventy-two - 1 1/2" squares (A6a)
- **Fourteen 5" wide strips. From these, cut:**
  * 220 - 2 1/2" x 5" (A3a, A4a, B3, B4, C2, C3)
  * Eighteen - 1 1/2" sq. (add to A6a)
- **Four 4 1/2" wide strips. From these, cut:**
  * Twenty-eight - 2 1/2" x 4 1/2" (B2)
  Stack this cut:
  * Sixty - 1 1/2" squares (add to A6a)
- **Twenty 2 1/2" wide strips. From this, cut:**
  * 318 - 2 1/2" squares (A1a, A2a, B1, B5a, B6, C1, C4a)
  * Thirty-two - 1 1/2" x 2 1/2" (B9, C6)
  * Twenty-one - 1 1/2" squares (add to A6a)
- **Six 1 1/2" wide strips. From these, cut:**
  * 149 - 1 1/2" squares (add to A6a)

▨ **FROM FABRIC II, CUT: (MED. GRAPE PRINT)**
- **Ten 5" wide strips. From these, cut:**
  * 160 - 2 1/2" x 5" (A3, A4)
- **Five 4 1/2" wide strips. From these, cut:**
  * Eighty - 2 1/2" x 4 1/2" (A2)
- **Eleven 2 1/2" wide strips. From these, cut:**
  * 170 - 2 1/2" squares (A5a, B1, B2a, C1)

■ **FROM FABRIC III, CUT: (DK. GRAPE TEXTURED PRINT)**
- **Two 9 1/2" wide strips. From these, cut:**
  * Thirty - 2 1/2" x 9 1/2" (B8, C7)
- **Two 7 1/2 wide strips. From these, cut:**

  * Thirty - 2 1/2" x 7 1/2" (B7, C5)
- **Five 6 1/2" wide strips. From these, cut:**
  * Thirty - 6 1/2" squares (B5, C4)
- **Four 5" wide strips. From these, cut:**
  * Sixty - 2 1/2" x 5" (B3a, B4a, C2a, C3a)
  * Eighteen - 1 1/2" squares (B6a, B9a, C6a)
- **Three 4 1/2" wide strips. From these, cut:**
  * Twenty - 4 1/2" squares (A1)
  Stack this cut:
  * Fifty-four - 1 1/2" sq. (add to 1 1/2" sq.)
- **Sixteen 2 1/2" wide strips. Eleven for straight-grain binding. From remainder, cut:**
  * Eighty - 2 1/2" squares (A6)
- **Five 1 1/2" wide strips. From these, cut:**
  * One - 1 1/2" x 40" (Q1)
  * Two - 1 1/2" x 31" (Q1) Piece to opposite short ends of 40" wide strip to = one 100 1/2" strip.
  * Forty-eight - 1 1/2" sq. (add to 1 1/2" sq.)

Block A Assembly

1. Block A is made the same as Block A for the throw. Refer to the diagrams and instructions for Block A on pages 69 and 70. Make 20 of Block A.

Rectrangles for blocks B and C

Making units B3, B4, C2, and C3. Make 28 of each for Block B. Make 2 of each for Block C.

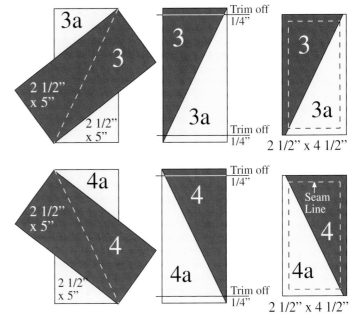

Assembly For Blocks B and C.

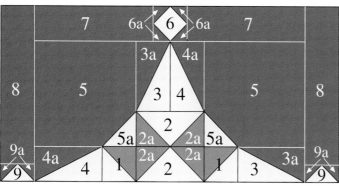

Block B. Make 14. When completed, block should measure 10 1/2" x 20 1/2".

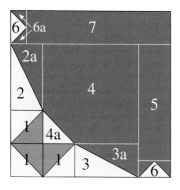

Block C. Make 2. When completed, block should measure 10 1/2" square.

1. The border of this quilt has two blocks; B and C blocks. The diagrams below show the Rectrangles to be made for the blocks. The instructions tell you how many units to make. Follow the diagrams to complete the Rectrangles. Refer to page 8 for making the Rectrangles.

2. These instructions are for one of Block B. Refer to Block B diagram and use diagonal corner technique to make two each of units 2, 5, and 9, and one of Unit 6.

Place 2 1/2" squares of fabrics I and II right sides facing and raw edges matchng. Stitch diagonal, trim seam, and press. Make 28 for Block B, and 6 for Block C.

3. Blocks B and C require triangle squares. Refer to the diagram at left and make the triangle squares as directed.

4. To assemble Block B, join units 3 and 4 as shown. Refer to the block diagram for correct position of the units. Join Unit 2 to the bottom of each combined 3-4 unit pairs. Join Unit 5, combined units 2-4, and Unit 5, carefully matching seams.

5. For the bottom row, join units 4, 1, 2, 1, and 3 in a horizontal row. Join this row to the bottom of the block, matching all seams.

6. For the top of the block, join units 7, 6, and 7 in a row. Join this row to the top of the block, matching star points. Join units 8 and 9. Make two. Join them to opposite sides of the block to complete it. Make 14 of Block B.

7. For Block C, join units 1 and 2; then add Unit 4 to the right side, matching diagonal corner seams. Join a pair of Unit 1's, and Unit 3. Add this row to the bottom of the block, again carefully matching seams.

8. Join units 5 and 6. Add these combined units to the right side of the block. Join units 6 and 7. Join these combined units to the top of the block to complete it. Make 2.

Quilt Assembly

1. To assemble the quilt, begin by joining four Block A's together in a horizontal row, carefully matching star points. Make five rows and join them together, matching star points and corner seams.

2. For the side borders, refer to the quilt diagram on the following page, and join five Block B's together in a row as shown. Make two rows. Join the rows to opposite sides of the quilt top, matching star points and corner seams. For the bottom border, join four B blocks in a row as shown, matching the bottom point seams. Refer to the quilt diagram for correct positioning of Block C, and join the corner Block C's to opposite short sides of the row. Make one. Join the row to the bottom of the quilt, again matching seams. Join previously pieced Unit Q1 to the quilt top to complete it.

3. This quilt has wonderful circular areas perfect for your best quilting to show up. For photography, we like the quilting in a color that will show up the best. I am getting accustomed to this, and I like it on some pieces. Mary used a silver metallic on the pillow and it is beautiful.

4. Make 460" of straight-grain binding from Fabric III, and bind your quilt. See page 13 for binding.

Quilt Assembly Diagram

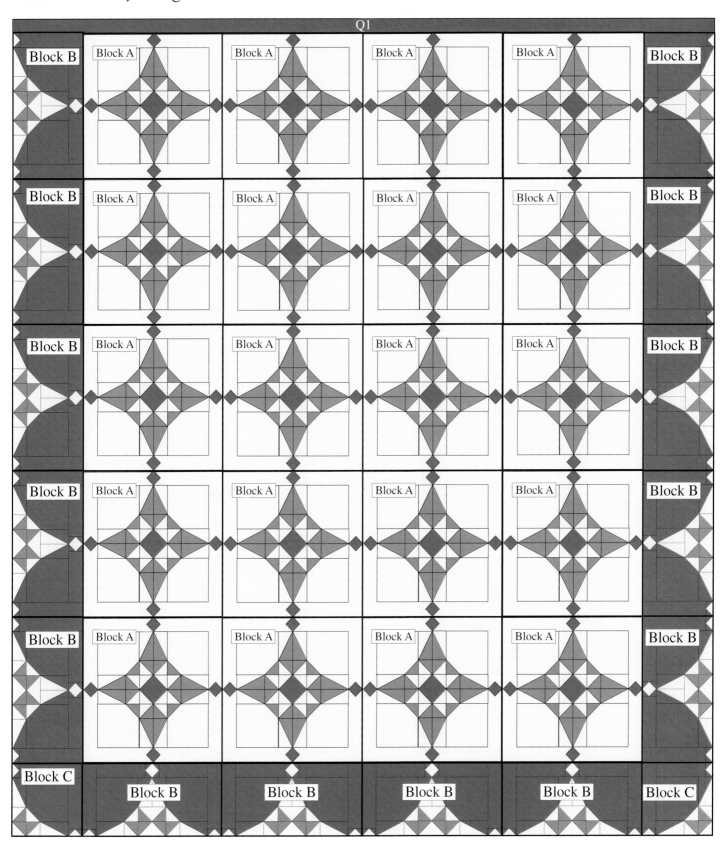

Jingle Bulls!

These baby Bulls are 5 weeks old! If you can imagine, there was another baby in the basket, beneath these little guys, and it was sound asleep! As you look through this book it is most likely after the Holidays. I am working on it prior to Thanksgiving. From the Bono Home to yours: May a quilt and a puppy or kitten keep you warm in every way, every day!

MATERIALS FOR TREE SKIRT

Fabric I (ivory with pine cone print)
Need 41"   1 3/8 yards
Fabric II (dark green dotted print)
Need 82"   2 1/2 yards
Fabric III (medium green swirl print)
Need 21"   3/4 yard
Fabric IV (light green textured print)
Need 21"   3/4 yard
Fabric V (dark brown print)
Need 19"   3/4 yard
Fabric VI (dark rust print)
Need 16"   5/8 yard
Fabric VII (honey tan print)
Need 4 1/2"   1/4 yard
Fabric VIII (bright red print)
Need 3 1/2" x 6 3/4" Scrap
Fabric IX (bright gold print)
Need 5 1/2" x 8 1/2" Scrap
Backing   3 1/2 yards

Tree skirt finishes to: 54 1/2" square.
Techniques used: Rectrangles.
Great Beginner Project!

CUTTING FOR TREE SKIRT

■ **FROM FABRIC I, CUT: (IVORY WITH PINE CONE PRINT)**
- **Four 7" wide strips. From these, cut:**
  - * Forty - 3 1/2" x 7" (A6, A7, A8, A9, C1, C2)
  - * Four - 1 1/2" squares (A1)
- **Two 6 1/2" wide strips. From these, cut:**
  - * Sixteen - 3 1/2" x 6 1/2" (A10)

■ **FROM FABRIC II, CUT: (DARK GREEN DOTTED PRINT)**
- **One 18" square to cut 2" wide bias binding.**
- **Six 7" wide strips. From these, cut:**
  - * Fifty-six - 3 1/2" x 7" (A6a, A7a, B1a, B2a, B3a, B4a)
  - Stack this cut lengthwise:
  - * Twelve - 3 1/2" x 5 1/2" (B7)
- **Two 3 1/2" wide strips. From these, cut:**
  - * Four - 3 1/2" x 5 1/2" (add to B7)
  - * Four - 3 1/2" squares (B5)
  - * Four - 2 1/2" x 3 1/2" (B8)
- **Six 2 1/2" wide strips for straight grain binding.**

■ **FROM FABRIC III, CUT: (MEDIUM GREEN SWIRL PRINT)**
- **Three 7" wide strips. From these, cut:**
  - * Thirty-two - 3 1/2" x 7" (A8a, A9a, B3, B4)

■ **FROM FABRIC IV, CUT: (LIGHT GREEN TEXTURED PRINT)**
- **Three 7" wide strips. From these, cut:**
  - * Twenty-four - 3 1/2" x 7" (B1, B2)
  - * Four - 3 1/2" x 6 1/2" (C10)

■ **FROM FABRIC V, CUT: (DARK BROWN PRINT)**
- **Two 9 1/2" wide strips. From these, cut:**
  - * Twelve - 3 1/2" x 9 1/2" (Q2)
  - * Eight - 3 1/2" x 7" (C1a, C2a)
  - * One - 6 1/2" square (Q1)
  - * Four - 1 1/2" x 2 1/2" (A4)
  - * Four - 1 1/2" squares (A2)

■ **FROM FABRIC VI, CUT: (DARK RUST PRINT)**
- **One 9 1/2" wide strip. From this, cut:**
  - * Eight - 3 1/2" x 9 1/2" (Q3)
  - Stack this cut vertically
  - * Eight - 2 3/4" x 3 7/8" (C9)
- **One 6 1/2" wide strip. From this, cut:**
  - * Four - 1 5/8" x 6 1/2" (C3)
  - Stack these cuts:
  - * Four - 2" squares (C6)
  - * Twelve - 1 1/4" x 2" (C4, C7)

■ **FROM FABRIC VII, CUT: (HONEY TAN PRINT)**
- **Three 1 1/2" wide strips. From these, cut:**
  - * Twenty-four - 1 1/2" x 3 1/2" (A5, B6)
  - * Four - 1 1/2" x 2 1/2" (A3)

■ **FROM FABRIC VIII, CUT: (BRIGHT RED PRINT)**
- **Four - 1 1/2" x 3 1/8" (C8)**

■ **FROM FABRIC IX, CUT: (BRIGHT GOLD PRINT)**
- **Eight - 2" squares (C5)**

Rectrangles For Blocks A, B, & C

1. For the Rectrangles on page 79, draw a line diagonally from one corner to the other. Place rectangles as shown in diagrams on page 79. Pin if necessary so that the Rectrangles do not slip.

2. Press the top Rectrangle over as shown. Trim top Rectrangles even with foundation unit if necessary. Trim 1/4" off at the top and bottom of each unit as shown.

3. The diagrams show how the Rectrangle should look at top and bottom when 1/4" is trimmed off. The dashed lines on the third diagrams show your seam allowance, and the measurement at the top gives you the size after trimming off the top and bottom. Make the required number of each Rectrangle shown. For more on making Rectrangles, refer to page 8.

Making Unit A6. Make 8.

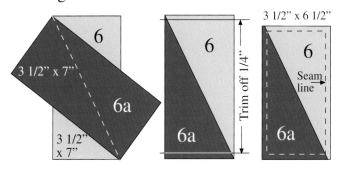

Making Unit A7. Make 8.

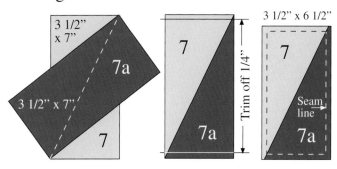

Making Unit A9. Make 8.

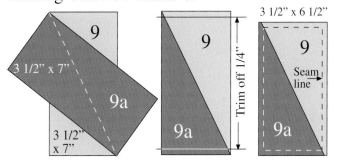

Making Unit A8. Make 8.

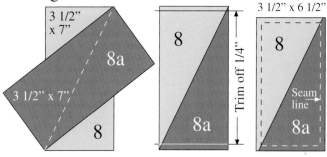

Making Unit B2. Make 12.

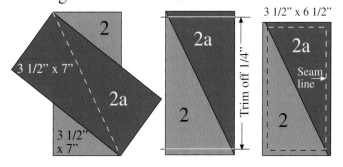

Making Unit B1. Make 12.

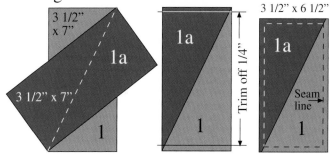

Making Unit B4. Make 8.

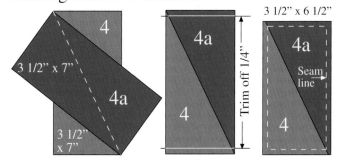

Making Unit B3. Make 8.

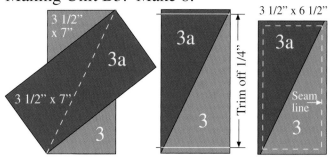

Making Unit C2. Make 4.

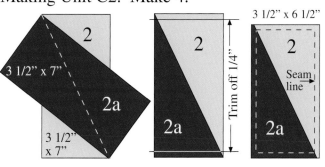

Making Unit C1. Make 4.

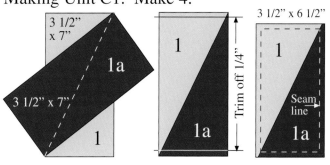

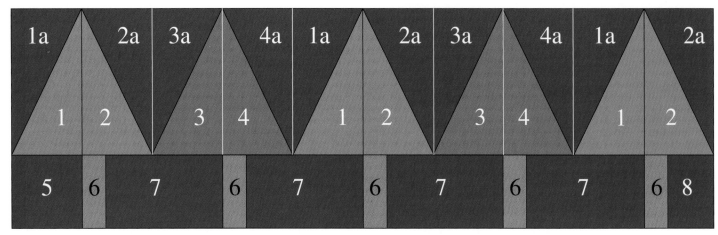

Block B, Make 4. When completed, block should measure 9 1/2" x 30 1/2".

Block A Assembly

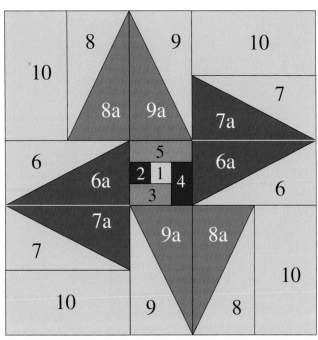

Block A, Make 4. When completed, block should measure 15 1/2" square.

1. To piece Block A, begin in the center, and join units 1 and 2; then add Unit 3 to the bottom of the 1-2 combined units. Join Unit 4 to the right side; then add Unit 5 to the top.
2. The block is put together in three rows. Beginning with the top row, join units 10, 8, and 9. Join units 10 and 7 as shown; then add them to the right side of combined units 8-10. Make two of these rows. One for the top row and one for the bottom. For the center row, refer to block diagram for correct placement, and join Unit 6 to opposite sides of previously pieced center.
3. Join the three rows together, carefully matching seams to complete Block A. Make 4.

Block B Assembly

1. Refer to Rectrangle diagrams on page 79. The instructions tell you how many units to make, and instruct you about what fabrics to use. Follow the diagrams to complete the Rectrangles.
2. To piece Block B, join the tree tops first. For this top row, join units 1, 2, 3, 4, 1, 2, 3, 4, 1, and 2 in a row, carefully matching points.
3. For the bottom tree trunk row, join units 5, 6, 7, 6, 7, 6, 7, 6, 7, 6, and 8 in a horizontal row. Join this row to the bottom of the trees, matching Unit 6 seams as shown. Make 4 of Block B.

Block C Assembly

1. Refer to Rectrangle diagrams on page 79 to make the roof. The instructions tell you how many units to make, and instruct you about what fabrics to use. Follow the diagrams to complete the Rectrangles.
2. To piece Block C, begin by joining units 1 and 2 as shown. For the house, join units 4, 5, 6, 5, and 4 in a horizontal row. Join Unit 3 to the top of this row. Join units 7 and 8; then add Unit 9 to opposite sides of the 7-8 combined units. Join Unit 10 to bottom of this row. Join this door row to the bottom of the window row, matching seams. Join the house bottom to the roof. Make 4 of Block C.

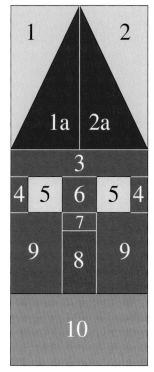

Block C, Make 4. When completed, block should measure 6 1/2" x 15 1/2".

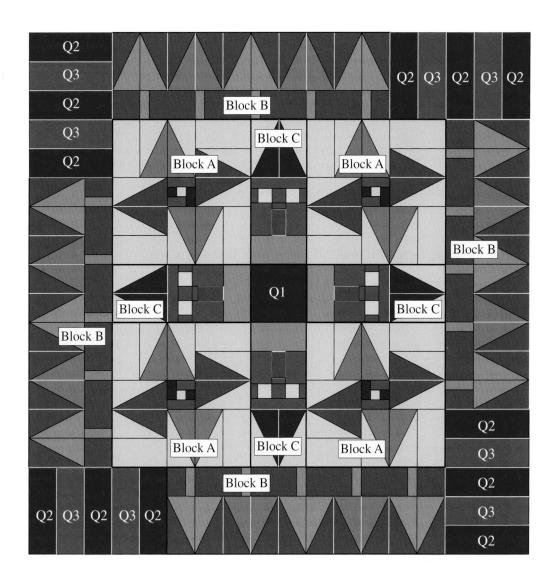

Tree Skirt Assembly

1. The tree skirt is assembled in rows. Follow these instructions, and refer frequently to the tree skirt diagram shown above. For the house/tree rows, join blocks A, C, and A in a row. Make 2 of these rows. For the center row, join Block C, Unit Q1, and Block C as shown. Join the three rows together, referring to the tree skirt diagram for correct placement.

2. For the top and bottom borders, join units Q2, and Q3. Join these combined units to the right side of Block B as shown. Make two of these rows, and join them to the top and bottom of the tree skirt.

3. For the tree skirt side borders, it will be important for you to refer to the diagram so that the "Q" units are going in the right direction. Beginning at the top left corner, join the five "Q" units as shown. Make two. Join these units to the right side of Block B as shown. Join units Q2, Q3, and Q2 as shown. Make two and add them to the left side of each Block B as shown. Join these rows to opposite sides of the tree skirt, matching corner seams.

4. Cut a 6" hole in the center of the tree skirt (Unit Q1); then cut a slit from the hole to one corner. To bind this section, you will need to cut an 18" square of Fabric II for the 2 1/2" wide bias binding. The straight edges of the tree skirt may be bound with straight-grain binding. Refer to page 13 for binding.

5. Quilt as desired, and bind your tree skirt.

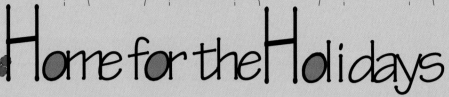 Home for the Holidays

The star in this holiday design is the same as the "Shooting Star" block in our sampler quilt. It is our version of the Ohio Star, and it worked so well and looked so different in other colors that we used it in two other projects. This ensemble is great for beginners, with quick and easy piecing.

Table Runner finishes to: 16 1/2" x 52 1/2".
Place Mats finish to: 16 1/2" x 20 1/2".
Techniques used: Rectrangles. strip sets, and diagonal corners.
Great Beginner Project!

MATERIALS FOR TABLE RUNNER

☐	**Fabric I (medium gold print)**	
	Need 21 1/2"	3/4 yard
☐	**Fabric II (dark gold print)**	
	Need 20"	3/4 yard
☐	**Fabric III (ivory print)**	
	Need 5"	1/4 yard
☐	**Fabric IV (Christmas green print)**	
	Need 7 1/2"	3/8 yard
☐	**Fabric V (dark red print)**	
	Need 9 1/2"	3/8 yard
	Backing	**1 5/8 yards**

CUTTING FOR TABLE RUNNER

FROM FABRIC I, CUT: (MEDIUM GOLD PRINT)
- Two 5" wide strips. From these, cut:
  * Twenty-four - 2 1/2" x 5" (A2, A3)
  * Eight - 2 1/2" x 4 1/2" (A4, Q4)
- Two 4 1/2" wide strips. From these, cut:
  * Twelve - 2 1/2" x 4 1/2" (add to above)
  * Two - 4 1/2" x 6 1/2" (Q1)
- One 2 1/2" wide strip for Strip Set 1

FROM FABRIC II, CUT: (DARK GOLD PRINT)
- Two 5" wide strips. From these, cut:
  * Twenty-four - 2 1/2" x 5" (A2a, A3a)
  * Three - 4 1/2" squares (A1)
- Four 2 1/2" wide strips for straight-grain binding

FROM FABRIC III, CUT: (IVORY PRINT)
- Two 2 1/2" wide strips. From these, cut:
  * Twenty-four - 2 1/2" squares (A2b, A3b)

FROM FABRIC IV, CUT: (XMAS GREEN PRINT)
- Three 2 1/2" wide strips. Two for Strip Sets 1 and 2. From remaining strip, cut:
  * Sixteen - 2 1/2" squares (Q3)

FROM FABRIC V, CUT: (DARK RED PRINT)
- One 4 1/2" wide strip for Strip Set 2.
- Two 2 1/2" wide strips. From these, cut:
  * Four - 2 1/2" x 6 1/2" (Q5)
  * Twenty - 2 1/2" squares (A1a, Q2)

83

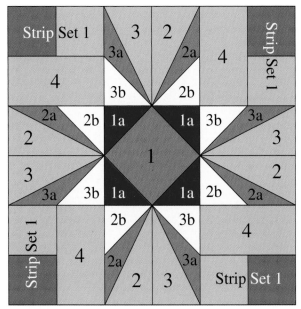

Block A. Make 3. When completed, block should measure 12 1/2" square.

Block A Assembly

1. These instructions are for one block. For the Rectrangles, draw a line diagonally from one corner to the other. Place rectrangles as shown in diagrams below. Pin if necessary so that the Rectrangles do not slip.

2. Press the top Rectrangle over as shown. Trim top Rectrangles even with foundation unit if necessary.

Strip Set 1. Make 1. Cut into twelve 2 1/2" segments.

Strip Set 2. Make 1. Cut into twelve 2 1/2" segments.

Trim 1/4" off at the top and bottom of each unit as shown.

3. The diagrams show how the Rectrangle should look at top and bottom when 1/4" is trimmed off. The diagonal corner is joined after trimming the unit as shown. The dashed lines on the diagram at right shows your seam allowance, and the measurement at the top gives you the size after trimming off the top and bottom. Make 12 of each Rectrangle.

4. Refer to the strip set diagrams above, and join the strips as directed. Cut into the specified number of segments. Refer to page 6 for making strip sets.

5. Use diagonal corner technique to make one of Unit 1.

6. The block is pieced in three rows. To begin, join units 2 and 3 as shown. Make four pair. Beginning at the top left corner, join Strip Set 1 and Unit 4. Make four. Referring to the block diagram for correct position of the units, join the combined Strip Set 1-Unit 4 combined units to opposite sides of the 2-3 combined Rectrangle pair. Make two of these rows.

7. For the center row, join the 2-3 Rectrangle pair to opposite sides of Unit 1 as shown. The points should be matched carefully. Again referring to the block diagram, join the three rows, carefully matching corner seams and star points to complete the block. Make three of Block A.

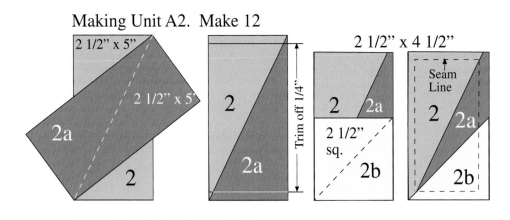

84

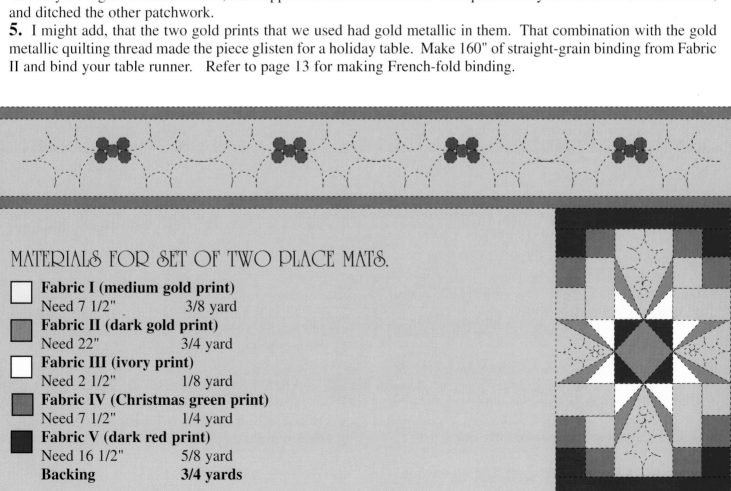

Table Runner Assembly

1. To assemble the table runner, join the rows between Block A first. To do so, join units 2, 3, 4, 3, and 2. Make two rows. Referring to the diagram above, join the two rows between the A blocks, matching seams where necessary.

2. For the outer side rows, again refer to the diagram above, and working from top to bottom, join two of Strip Set 2 together as shown. Join these combined strip set segments to the top of Unit 1. Once again join two Strip Set 2 segments, referring to diagram for correct placement of the strip set segments. Join these combined strip sets to the bottom of Unit 1. Make two of these combined units. Join to opposite ends of the A blocks.

3. For the top and bottom rows, join Unit 2, Strip Set 2, units 3, 4, 3, 5, 3, 4, 3, 5, 3, 4, 3, Strip Set 2, and Unit 2 in a horizontal row. Make two and join to top and bottom of table runner, carefully matching seams.

4. Mary used gold metallic thread, and stippled in the Fabric I areas. She quilted holly leaves in the dark red areas, and ditched the other patchwork.

5. I might add, that the two gold prints that we used had gold metallic in them. That combination with the gold metallic quilting thread made the piece glisten for a holiday table. Make 160" of straight-grain binding from Fabric II and bind your table runner. Refer to page 13 for making French-fold binding.

MATERIALS FOR SET OF TWO PLACE MATS.

	Fabric		
☐	**Fabric I (medium gold print)**	Need 7 1/2"	3/8 yard
☐	**Fabric II (dark gold print)**	Need 22"	3/4 yard
☐	**Fabric III (ivory print)**	Need 2 1/2"	1/8 yard
☐	**Fabric IV (Christmas green print)**	Need 7 1/2"	1/4 yard
☐	**Fabric V (dark red print)**	Need 16 1/2"	5/8 yard
	Backing		**3/4 yards**

CUTTING FOR SET OF TWO PLACE MATS.

☐ **FROM FABRIC I, CUT: (MEDIUM GOLD PRINT)**
• Three 2 1/2" wide strips. Two for strip sets 1 and 2. From remaining strip, cut:
    * Four - 2 1/2" squares (6)

☐ **FROM FABRIC II, CUT: (DARK GOLD PRINT)**
• One 5" wide strip. From this, cut:
    * Sixteen - 2 1/2" x 5" (2a, 3a)
• One 4 1/2" wide strip. From this, cut:
    * Two - 4 1/2" squares (1)
• Five 2 1/2" wide strips for straight-grain binding.

Refer to page 12 for making double sided napkins.

☐ **FROM FABRIC III, CUT: (IVORY PRINT)**
• One 2 1/2" wide strip. From this, cut:
    * Sixteen - 2 1/2" squares (2b, 3b)

☐ **FROM FABRIC IV, CUT: (XMAS GREEN PRINT)**
• Three 2 1/2" wide strips. One for Strip Set 1. From remaining strips, cut:
    * Eight - 2 1/2" x 4 1/2 (7)
    * Eight - 2 1/2" squares (1a)

FROM FABRIC V, CUT: (DARK RED PRINT)

- **One 5" wide strip.** From this, cut:
  - * Sixteen - 2 1/2" x 5" (2, 3)
- **Two 4 1/2" wide strips.** From these, cut:
  - * Two - 4 1/2" x 6 1/2" (8)
  - * Fourteen - 2 1/2" x 4 1/2" (4)
  - * Four - 2 1/2" squares (5)
- **One 2 1/2" wide strip for Strip Set 2.**

Place Mat Assembly

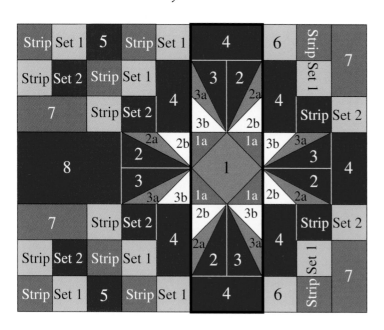

Making unit A2, and A3. Make 8 of each.

The Rectrangles below are made the same as for the table runner. The only difference is the color, and the number of units that you need to make. Refer to page 84 for complete construction diagrams for these units.

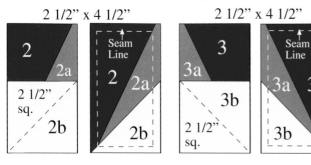

2 1/2" x 4 1/2"   2 1/2" x 4 1/2"

Strip Set 1. Make 1.
Cut into sixteen
2 1/2" segments

Strip Set 2. Make 1.
Cut into twelve
2 1/2" segments

1. The Rectrangles for the place mats are made the same as for the table runner. Follow those diagrams and instructions, and the color changes below left.

2. Refer to the strip set diagrams below, and join the strips as directed. Cut into the specified number of segments. Use diagonal corner technique to make one of Unit 1.

3. The place mat is assembled differently than the Star block for the table runner. The Star for the place mats must be assembled in three different sections. Beginning with the left side section, join Strip Set 1, Strip Set 2, and Unit 7 in a vertical row. Join Unit 5 and Strip Set 1. Join Strip Set 1, and Strip Set 2; then add Unit 4 to the right side of the combined strip set segments. Join the combined Unit 5, Strip Set 1 combination to the top as shown. Join these two sections together, referring to place mat diagram for correct placement.

4. Join units 2 and 3; then add Unit 8 to the left side of these combined units. Join these units to the bottom of the previously joined units.

5. Join Unit 7, Strip Set 2, and Strip Set 1 in a vertical row. Join Strip Set 2, and Strip Set 1; then add Unit 4 to the right side of the combined strip set segments. Join Unit 5, and Strip Set 1. Add these to the bottom of the Strip Set 2/Strip Set 1/Unit 4 combination. Join the two strip set sections together; then add them to the bottom of combined units 2-3- and 8 to complete the left side section.

6. For the center section, join units 3 and 2; then add Unit 4 to the top. Make two. Join the two star point combined units to the top and bottom of Unit 1 as shown to complete the center section.

7. For the right side section, join units 6 and 4. Join Strip Set 1 and Unit 7; then add Strip Set 2 to the bottom, matching seams. Join combined units 6-4 to the left side of the strip set combined units. Join units 3 and 2; then add Unit 4 to the right side of these combined units. Join these units to the bottom of the previously joined strip set units. Join units 4 and 6. Join Strip Set 1 and Unit 7; then add Strip Set 2 to the top of this combination, matching seams. Join the combined 4-6 units to the left side, again matching seams. Join this combination to the bottom of the other combined units to complete the right side section. Join the three sections together, carefully matching seams to complete the place mat.

8. Mary used gold metallic thread to quilt the place mats. She stippled the background behind the star, and quilted holly leaves in the green spaces.

9. Make 80" of straight-grain binding for each place mat, and bind. Refer to page 13 for binding.

Clark Hybrid

This lovely flower wall piece by Susan Clark can be the center of attention in your home, or as a gift for a special friend. Before we added the loop at the top, we placed it in the center of a table, and it was gorgeous! A design of many uses, it could also be used as a pillow. Change the flower colors, and have a set of throw pillows for bed, sofa or chair.

Flower block finishes to: 27 1/2" square.
Techniques used: Rectrangles, and diagonal corners.

MATERIALS FOR FLOWER

Fabric I (burgundy print)
Need 22 1/2"   3/4 yard

Fabric II (medium rose print)
Need 8 7/8"   3/8 yard

Fabric III (bright pink print)
Need 2 1/2"   1/8 yard

Fabric IV (light green print)
Need 9 3/4"   3/8 yard

Fabric V (medium green print)
Need 3 1/2"   1/4 yard

Fabric VI (dark green print)
Need 1 7/8"   1/8 yard

Fabric VII (medium yellow print)
Need 5" square   Scrap
Backing   1 yard

CUTTING FOR FLOWER

 FROM FABRIC I, CUT: (BURGUNDY PRINT)
- One 4 1/2" wide strip. From this, cut:
    * Four - 4 1/2" squares (4)
    * One - 1 1/2" x 4" (loop for hanging)
- Four 2 1/2" wide strips. Three for straight-grain binding. From remaining strip, cut:
    * Eight - 2 1/2" x 5" (2a, 3a)
- Four 2" wide strips. From these, cut:
    * Two - 2" x 27 1/2" (16)
    * Two - 2" x 24 1/2" (15)

FROM FABRIC II, CUT: (MEDIUM ROSE PRINT)
- One 2 1/2" wide strip. From this, cut:
    * Eight - 2 1/2" squares (1a, 4b)
    * One 2 1/8" x 13 1/4" (12)
- Three 2 1/8" wide strips. From these, cut:
    * One 2 1/8" x 13 1/4" (add to 12 above)
    * Two - 2 1/8" x 11 3/4" (11)
    * Two - 2 1/8" x 11 5/8" (14)
    * Two - 2 1/8" x 10 1/8" (13)

FROM FABRIC III, CUT: (BRIGHT PINK PRINT)
- One 2 1/2" wide strip. From this, cut:
    * Eight - 2 1/2" x 5" (2, 3)

FROM FABRIC IV, CUT: (LIGHT GREEN PRINT)
- Two 4 7/8" wide strips. From these, cut:
    * Two - 4 7/8" x 8 3/4" (10)
    * Two - 4 7/8" x 8 5/8" (9)
    * Two - 4 3/8" x 4 7/8" (7)
    * Two - 4 1/4" x 4 7/8" (8)
    * Four - 2 1/2" squares (4a)
    From scrap, cut:
    * Eight - 1 7/8" squares (5a, 6a)
    * Four - 1 1/8" squares (5b)
    * Four - 1" squares (6b)

FROM FABRIC V, CUT: (MEDIUM GREEN PRINT)
- One 3 1/2" wide strip. From this, cut:
    * Four - 3 1/2" x 4 7/8" (5)
    * Eight - 2 1/8" squares (2b, 12a, 14a)
    From scrap, cut:
    * Four - 1 1/4" x 2 1/8" (3b)

FROM FABRIC VI, CUT: (DARK GREEN PRINT)
- One 1 7/8" wide strip. From this, cut:
    * Four - 1 7/8" x 4 7/8" (6)
    * Four - 1 3/8" x 2 1/8" (3b)

FROM FABRIC VII, CUT: (YELLOW PRINT)
- One - 4 1/2" square (1)

Block Assembly

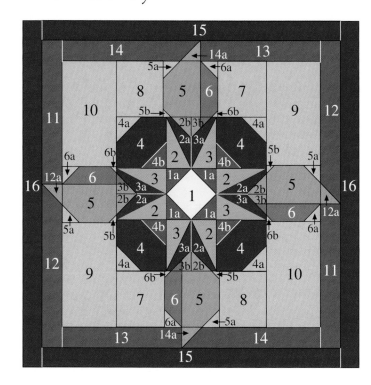

1. For the Rectrangles, refer to diagrams and instructions on page 91. The Rectrangles for Unit 2 have a diagonal corner from Fabric V. The Rectrangles for Unit 3 utilize a small strip set for the diagonal corner. Refer to the instructions with the diagrams to make the small strip set. The diagrams show how to place the strip set diagonal corner. Make four of each unit. For more information about making the Rectrangles, turn to page 8.

2. Use diagonal corner technique to make four of units 4, 5, and 6, two each of units 12 and 14, and one of Unit 1.

3. To piece the flower, refer to the block diagram above, and join units 2 and 3. Make four pair. Once again referring to the block diagram for correct placement of diagonal corners, join Unit 4 to opposite sides of one combined 2-3 pairs. Make two.

4. For the flower center, join two 2-3 pairs to opposite sides of Unit 1. Join the flower top and bottom

Making units 2 and 3. Make 4 of each.

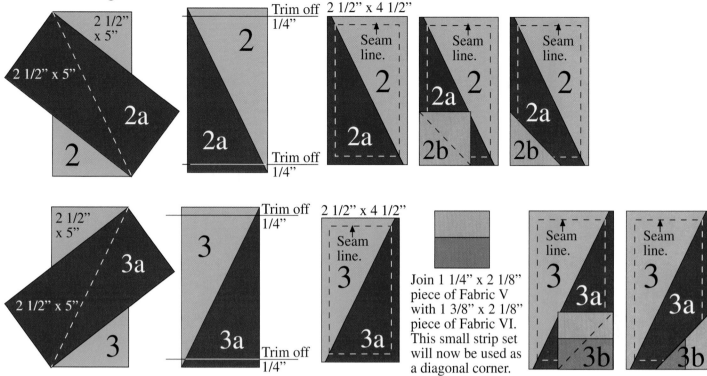

sections to the top and bottom of the flower center section, matching seams.

5. Join units 8, 5, 6, and 7 in a horizontal row. Make 2. Join the rows to top and bottom of flower, turning the bottom row as shown in block diagram. Carefully match the leaf seams.   Join units 10, 6, 5, and 9 in a vertical row. Make 2. Join the rows to opposite sides of the flower, turning one row as shown.

6. For the borders, join units 13 and 14. Make 2. Join to the top and bottom of the block, turning the bottom combined units to match the leaf seams. Join units 11 and 12. Make 2. Join to opposite sides of the block, turning one, and matching leaf seams. Join Unit 15 to the top of bottom of the block; then add Unit 16 to the sides to complete the block.

Quilting & Finishing

1. Mary did some outstanding things with this block. We all decided that the block looked best on point for hanging on a wall. Mary used silver and gold metallic thread. She quilted small circles in the yellow flower center, and diagonal lines on the pink petals that followed the contour of the petal. There are swirls that curl at the ends coming out of the burgundy petals, and the light green open areas have feather quilting in them.

She used gold metallic on the leaves, and made a curved line for the leaf veins; then small lines, that followed the contour of the leaf, were quilted about 3/8" apart. The borders are quilted with feathers.

2. Use three strips of Fabric I and make straight-grain binding. Bind the block. Refer to page 13 for French-fold binding.

3. A sleeve was made for the back of the piece which goes from point to point, allowing us to insert a yard-stick to keep the block straight when it is hung. A 4 1/2" wide x 33" long piece of backing fabric was cut. Hem the short ends and top stitch the hem in place. Fold the sleeve in half lengthwise, right sides together, and stitch. Turn sleeve right side out and slip stitch in place on the backing.

4. Using the 1 1/2" x 4" scrap of Fabric I, make a small hem on the short ends, and top stitch in place. Fold the piece in half lengthwise, right sides together. Stitch, turn right side out, and make a loop. Slip stitch the loop in place on one corner in the back for hanging.

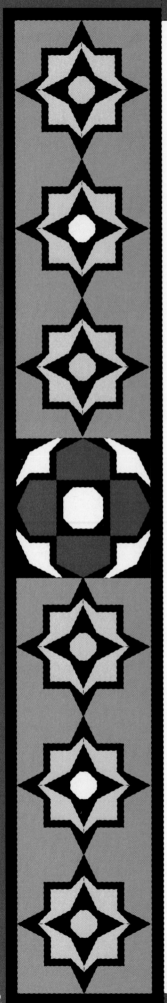

Stained Glass

Although we have never done a Stained Glass quilt, I have always been fascinated when my friends make stained glass wall quilts with bias tape.

I wasn't sure that a pieced wall quilt would work, but when Mary sent it back quilted, and we hung it in our picture window for the photo, I was extremely pleased with the results. Even though we have southwest furnishings in our home, I was very tempted to leave it in the window!

Wall quilt finishes to: 43 1/2" square. Techniques used: Rectrangles, diagonal corners, and Rectrangles with diagonal corners.

MATERIALS FOR QUILT

Fabric I (solid black)
Need 56 1/2"   1 3/4 yards

Fabric II (red batik)
Need 14"   1/2 yard

Fabric III (dark turquoise batik)
Need 7"   3/8 yard

Fabric IV (light turquoise batik)
Need 3 1/2"   1/4 yard

Fabric V (medium purple batik)
Need 9 1/2"   3/8 yard

Fabric VI (yellow batik)
Need 8 1/2"   3/8 yard

Fabric VII (pink batik)
Need 15"   5/8 yard
Backing   2 1/4 yards

CUTTING FOR QUILT

■ **FROM FABRIC I, CUT: (SOLID BLACK)**
- **Four 5" wide strips. From these cut**
  - * Sixty - four - 2 1/2" x 5" (A2a, A3a, A4a, A5a, A11a, A12a, A14a, A15a, A17a, A18a, A19a, A20a, B2a, B3a, B4a, B5a, B11a, B12a, B14a, B15a, B17a, B18a, B19a, B20a)

- Five 2 1/2" wide strips. For straight-grain binding.
- **Six 2" wide strips. From these, cut:**
  - * Two - 2" x 40 1/2" (Q1)
  - * Four - 2" x 22" (Q2) Piece two together to = two 43 1/2" lengths.
  - * Thirty-two - 2" squares (A1a, A21a, A22a, A23a, B1a, B21a, B22a, B23a)

- **Eight 1 1/2" wide strips. From these, cut:**
  * Thirty-two - 1 1/2" x 4 1/2" (A9, A25, B9, B25)
  * Thirty-two - 1 1/2" x 3 1/2" (A8, A24, B8, B24)
  * Thirty-two - 1 1/2" squares (A2b, A3b, A4b, A5b, B2b, B3b, B4b, B5b)

FROM FABRIC II, CUT: (RED BATIK)
- **One 5" wide strip. From this, cut:**
  * Sixteen - 2 1/2" x 5" (A12, A14, A15, A19, B12, B14, B15, B19)
- **Two 4 1/2" wide strips. From these, cut:**
  * Sixteen - 4 1/2" squares (A13, B13)

FROM FABRIC III, CUT: (DK. TURQUOISE BATIK)
- **One 2 1/2" wide strip. From this, cut:**
  * Eight - 2 1/2" x 5" (A17, A20, B17, B20)
- **One 4 1/2" wide strip. From this, cut:**
  * Eight - 4 1/2" squares (A16, B16)

FROM FABRIC IV, CUT: (LT. TURQUOISE BATIK)
- **One 3 1/2" wide strip. From this, cut:**
  * Four - 3 12" squares (A23, B23)

FROM FABRIC V, CUT: (MEDIUM PURPLE BATIK)
- **One 5" wide strip. From this, cut:**
  * Eight - 2 1/2" x 5" (A11, A18, B11, B18)
  * Four - 4 1/2" squares (A1, A10, B1, B10)
- **One 4 1/2" wide strip. From this, cut:**
  * Eight - 4 1/2" squares (add to 4 1/2" squares)

FROM FABRIC VI, CUT: (YELLOW BATIK)
- **One 5" wide strip. From this, cut:**
  * Eight - 2 1/2" x 5" (A4, A5, B4, B5)
  * Five - 3 1/2" squares (A7, A22, B7, B22)
  Stack this cut:
  * Six - 1 1/2" squares (A12b, A15b, B12b, B15b)
- **One 3 1/2" wide strip. From this, cut:**
  * Seven - 3 1/2" squares (add to 3 1/2" sq.)
  * Two - 1 1/2" squares (add to 1 1/2" sq.)

FROM FABRIC VII, CUT: (PINK BATIK)
- **Two 5" wide strips. From these, cut:**
  * Twenty-four - 2 1/2" x 5" (A2, A3, B2, B3)
  * Five - 3 1/2" squares (A6, A21, B6, B21)
- **One 3 1/2" wide strip. From this, cut:**
  * Eleven - 3 1/2" squares (add to 3 1/2" sq.)

- **One 1 1/2" wide strip. From this, cut:**
  * Twenty-four - 1 1/2" squares (A11b, A14b, A17b, A18b, A19b, A20b, B11b, B14b, B17b, B18b, B19b, B20b)

Assembly Of Mirror Image Blocks A & B.

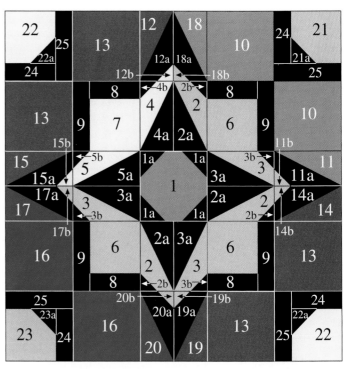

Block A. Make 2. When completed, block should measure 20 1/2" square.

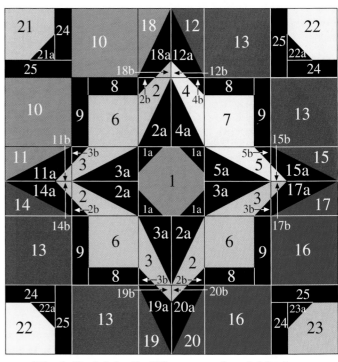

Block B. Make 2. When completed, block should measure 20 1/2" square.

Rectrangles For Blocks A & B

1. For the Rectrangles on pages 95 through 97, draw a line diagonally from one corner to the other. Place rectrangles as shown in diagrams at right. Pin if necessary so that the Rectrangles do not slip.

2. Press the top Rectrangle over as shown. Trim top Rectrangles even with foundation unit if necessary. Trim 1/4" off at the top and bottom of each unit as shown.

3. The diagrams show how the Rectrangle should look at top and bottom when 1/4" is trimmed off. The dashed lines on the third diagrams show your seam allowance, and the measurement at the top gives you the size after trimming off the top and bottom. Make the required number of each Rectrangle shown. For more on making Rectrangles, refer to page 8.

A Block Rectrangles

Making Unit A2. Make 3.

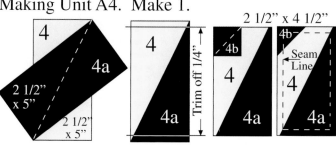

Making Unit A3. Make 3.

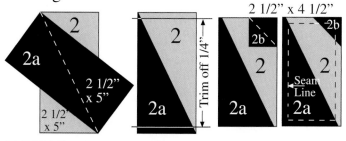

Making Unit A4. Make 1.

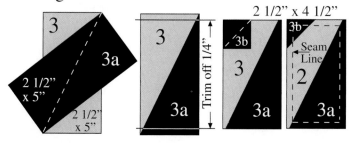

Making Unit A5. Make 1.

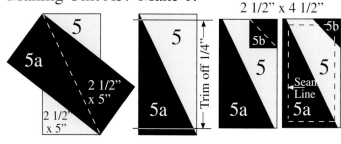

Making Unit A11. Make 1.

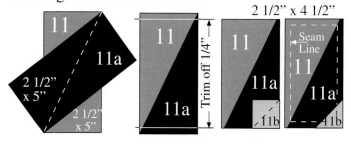

Making Unit A12. Make 1.

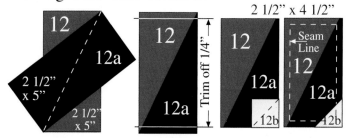

Making Unit A14. Make 1.

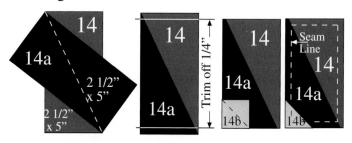

Making Unit A15. Make 1.

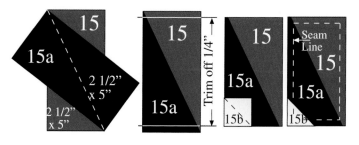

Making Unit A17. Make 1.

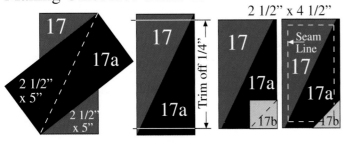

Making Unit A18. Make 1.

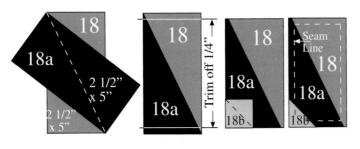

Making Unit A19. Make 1.

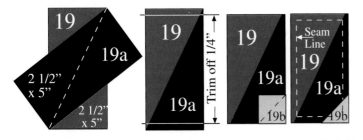

Making Unit A20. Make 1.

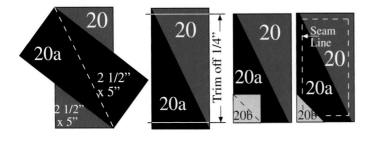

B Block Rectrangles

Making Unit B2. Make 3.

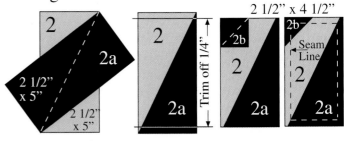

Making Unit B3. Make 3.

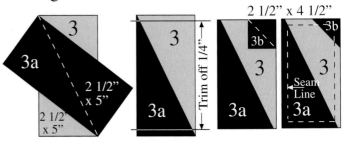

Making Unit B4. Make 1.

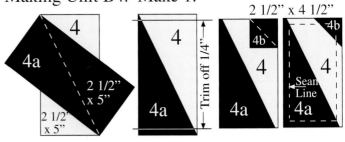

Making Unit B5. Make 1.

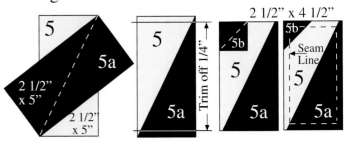

Making Unit B11. Make 1.

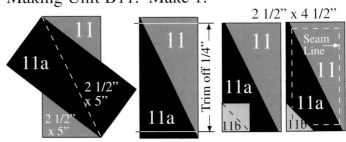

Making Unit B12. Make 1.

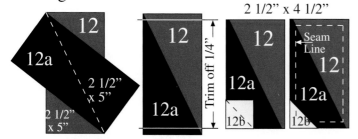

2 1/2" x 4 1/2"

Making Unit B14. Make 1.

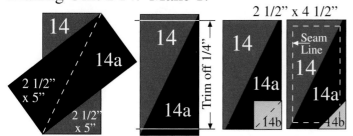

2 1/2" x 4 1/2"

Making Unit B15. Make 1.

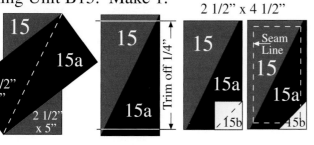

2 1/2" x 4 1/2"

Making Unit B17. Make 1.

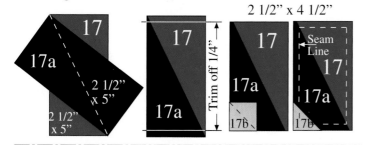

2 1/2" x 4 1/2"

Making Unit B18. Make 1.

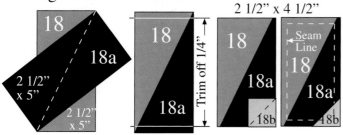

2 1/2" x 4 1/2"

Making Unit B19. Make 1.

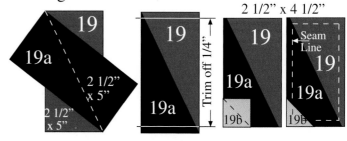

2 1/2" x 4 1/2"

Making Unit B20. Make 1.

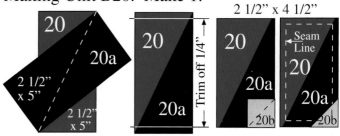

2 1/2" x 4 1/2"

Assembly For Mirror Image Blocks A & B.

1. For the Rectrangles, refer to diagrams and instructions on pages 95 through 97. The diagrams and directions show you the Rectrangle units to be made for each block and the fabrics to make them from. As the blocks and units are mirror images, the slant of the Rectrangles is also shown.   The Rectrangles on these pages have diagonal corners added after the initial Rectrangle unit is made. The diagonal corner colors are also shown in the diagrams. For more information about making Rectrangles, turn to page 8.

2. Use the diagonal corner technique to make two of unit 22, and one of units 1, 21, and 23 for each block.

3. These assembly instructions are for one of Block A, however Block B is made the same way, only it is a mirror image. Use these instructions, and refer to the diagrams of both blocks frequently for correct placement of all units. For more ease in piecing the blocks, we have divided them into five sections, beginning with the top row.

4. Beginning in the top left corner, join units 22 and 24; then add Unit 25 to the side of these combined units. Join units 13, 12, 18, and 10, in a horizontal row. Join units 21 and 24; then add Unit 25 to the bottom of these combined units. Join the 22-25 units to the left side of the horizontal row, and combined units 21-25 to the right side as shown to complete the first row.

5. For row two, join units 7 and 8; then add Unit 9 to the left side. Join Unit 13 to the left side of these combined units. Join units 4 and 2, matching seams; then add them to the right side of the other combined units. Join units 6 and 8; then add Unit 9 to right side. Make 2, one for Row 4. Join Unit 10 to Unit 9 and add these combined units to the right side of other combined units to complete Row 2.

6. For the center row, join units 15 and 17, carefully matching point seams. Join units 5 and 3, again matching seams. Join these combined units together, matching point seams. Join units 3 and 2. Join units 11 and 14. Join the combined 3-2 units to the 11-14 units, carefully matching points. Refer to the block diagram and join the combined 3, 5, 15 and 17 units to the left side of Unit 1; then join the remaining combined units to the right side of Unit 1 to complete the row.

7. For Row 4, join Unit 16 to the left side of previously pieced units 6-9. Join units 2 and 3, matching points. Join units 6 and 8; then add Unit 9 to right side. Join Unit 13 to Unit 9. Join the 6, 8, 9, and 16 combined units to the left side of combined units 2-3, and the remaining combined units to the right side as shown.

8. For bottom Row 5, begin by joining units 23 and 24; then add Unit 25 to the top of these combined units. Join Unit 16 to the right side. Join units 20 and 19, matching points; then add Unit 13 to the right side of Unit 19. Join these combined units to combined units 16-23-25. Join units 22 and 24; then add Unit 25 to the left side. Join this combination to the right side of the row to complete it.

9. Join the five rows together. Corner and point seams will need to be matched carefully. Don't be afraid to pin! Make 2 of Block A, and 2 of Block B.

Quilt Assembly

1. To assemble the quilt, refer to the diagram above and join blocks B and A as shown, carefully matching seams. Join blocks A and B as shown, again matching seams. Join the top and bottom sections together as shown. Join Unit Q1 to top and bottom of the quilt top; then add previously pieced Unit Q2 to opposite sides to complete the quilt top.

2. Mary used silver metallic thread to quilt most of this piece. Feather designs were quilted in the colored areas. On the points, straight lines were quilted to follow the contour of the pointed spaces. On the other black areas, Mary used black thread and stippled.

3. Use five 2 1/2" wide strips from Fabric I to make straight-grain binding. Refer to page 13 for binding.

Set the table with a Rectrangle!

This place mat set is not only attractive and functional, but it is easy to make, with large pieces. Only four fabrics are used for the traditional blocks that have a brand new look by using Rectrangles! We have even given new names to some of the old traditions. A bright look for your table, or a great gift for a friend.

Place mats finish to: 16 1/2" x 20 1/2".
Techniques used: Rectrangles, diagonal corners. and Rectrangles with diagonal corners.

MATERIALS FOR FOUR PLACE MATS

Fabric I (dark teal print)
Need 57 1/2"   1 3/4 yards
Fabric II (medium teal print)
Need 24"   3/4 yard
Fabric III (medium green batik)
Need 26"   7/8 yard
Fabric IV (pale green print)
Need 11 1/2"   1/2 yard
* Backing   1 1/2 yards

* We used dark teal for the backing.
If you choose to use this fabric, we
suggest purchasing 3 1/4 yards.

CUTTING FOR RADIANT STAR PLACE MAT

■ FROM FABRIC I, CUT: (DARK TEAL PRINT)
• One 5" wide strip. From this, cut:
  * Eight - 2 1/2" x 5" (2a, 3a)
  * One - 4 1/2" square (1)
  * Six - 2 1/2" x 4 1/2" (8)
• Three 2 1/2" wide strips. Two for straight-grain binding. From remaining strip, cut:
  * Six - 2 1/2" squares (7)

■ FROM FABRIC II, CUT: (MEDIUM TEAL PRINT)
• Two 2 1/2" wide strips. From these, cut:
  * Twenty-four - 2 1/2" squares (1a, 5)

■ FROM FABRIC III, CUT: (MEDIUM GREEN BATIK)
• One 5" wide strip. From this, cut:
  * Eight - 2 1/2" x 5" (2, 3)
  * One - 4 1/2" x 6 1/2" (9)
  * Three - 2 1/2" x 4 1/2" (4)
• One 2 1/2" wide strip. From this, cut:
  * Ten - 2 1/2" squares (6)

□ FROM FABRIC IV, CUT: (PALE GREEN PRINT
• One 2 1/2" wide strip. From this, cut:
  * Eight - 2 1/2" squares (2b, 3b)

Refer to page 12 for making double sided napkins.

Radiant Star Place Mat Assembly

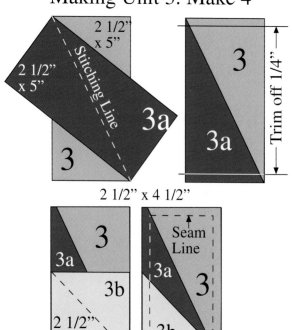

For this place mat you will need: 12 1/2" of Fabric I, 5" of Fabric II, 7 1/2" of Fabric III, and 2 1/2" of Fabric IV. Need 20 1/2" x 24 1/2" for backing.

1. For the Rectrangles, draw a line diagonally from one corner to the other. Place rectrangles as shown in diagrams at right. Pin if necessary so that the Rectrangles do not slip.

2. Press the top Rectrangle over as shown. Trim top Rectrangles even with foundation unit if necessary. Trim 1/4" off at the top and bottom of each unit as shown.

3. The diagrams show how the Rectrangle should look at top and bottom when 1/4" is trimmed off. The diagonal corner is joined after trimming the unit as shown. The dashed lines on the bottom diagrams show your seam allowance, and the measurement at the top gives you the size after trimming off the top and bottom. Make 4 of each Rectrangle. For more on making Rectrangles, refer to page 8.

4. Use diagonal corner technique to make one of Unit 1.

5. The place mat is assembled in three sections. Beginning with the left section, join units 8 and 5. Join units 7, 5, and 6 in a row. Join this row to the first row, matching seams. Join units 5, 6, and 5. Make four of these rows. Join one to the previous row, again matching seams. Join units 2 and 3 as shown. Make four pairs. Join Unit 4 to the pointed end of three of the pairs. Join one pair to bottom of 5-6-5 combined units; then add

another combined 5-6-5 unit row to the bottom of the star point combined units. Join units 5 and 6. Join units 7 and 5. Join these two combined unit combinations together as shown; then add Unit 8 to the left side. Join these combined units to the bottom of combined 5-6-5 units to complete the left side section.

6. For the center section, refer to place mat diagram for correct position of the units, and join two of the 2-4 star point pairs to the top and bottom of Unit 1.

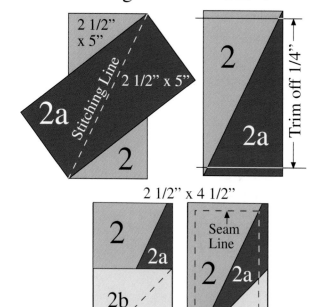

Making Unit 2. Make 4

Making Unit 3. Make 4

Radiant Star Assembly Continued

7. For the right section, join units 5 and 7. Make four. Join units 6 and 5. Make four. Join these two combined units together, matching seams. Join Unit 8 to the right side of these combined units; then add previously pieced combined 5-6-5 units to the bottom, again matching seams. For the top right corner, refer to place mat diagram on page 101 and join combined units 5-6 with combined units 7-5 as shown; then add Unit 8 to the bottom of these combined units. Join this corner section to other combined units as shown.

Join the remaining 2-3 pair to Unit 9 as shown. Join to the bottom of the pieced top section, matching seams. For the bottom of this section, join previously pieced 5-6-5 combined units to the left side of Unit 8. Join previously pieced 5-6 units to 5-7 combined units, matching seams. Make two. Join Unit 8 to the right side of one 5-6/5-7 combination. Join remaining 5-6/5-7 combined units to the right side of Unit 8; Join this section to the bottom of the 5-6-5-8 row, matching seams. Join to combined star point units to complete the right section.

8. Join the three sections together as shown in place mat diagram, matching all seams to complete the place mat top.

Quilting and Finishing

1. Mary used a mixture of matching thread and gold metallic thread to quilt this place mat. She quilted a Cathedral Window, curved look inside of the squares, and used feather motifs in gold metallic inside the open green areas. The patchwork was "ditched."

2. Use two 2 1/2" wide strips of Fabric I to bind your place mat. Refer to page 13 for French-fold binding.

CUTTING FOR GOONEY BIRDS PLACE MAT

■ **FROM FABRIC I, CUT: (DARK TEAL PRINT)**
- **One 5" wide strip. From this, cut:**
  * Fourteen - 2 1/2" x 5" (1a, 2a)
- **Two 2 1/2" wide strips for straight-grain binding.**
- **Three 1 1/2" wide strips. From these, cut:**
  * Two - 1 1/2" x 20 1/2" (5)
  * Three - 1 1/2" x 14 1/2" (3)

■ **FROM FABRIC II, CUT: (MEDIUM TEAL PRINT)**
- **One 9 1/2" wide strip. From this, cut:**
  * One - 9 1/2" x 14 1/2" (4)

■ **FROM FABRIC III, CUT: (MEDIUM GREEN BATIK)**
- **One 5" wide strip. From this, cut:**
  * Fourteen - 2 1/2" x 5" (1, 2)

Goony Birds Place Mat Assembly

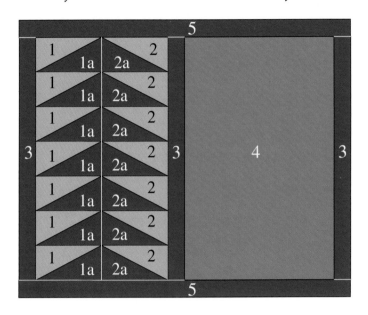

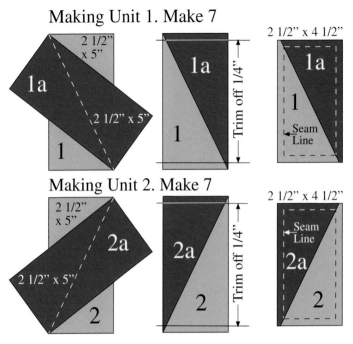

Making Unit 1. Make 7

Making Unit 2. Make 7

For this place mat you will need: 14 1/2" of Fabric I, 9 1/2" of Fabric II, and 5" of Fabric III. Need 20 1/2" x 24 1/2" for backing.

1. For the Rectrangles, draw a line diagonally from one corner to the other. Place rectrangles as shown in diagrams at right. Pin if necessary so that the Rectrangles do not slip.

2. Press the top Rectrangle over as shown. Trim top Rectrangles even with foundation unit if necessary. Trim 1/4" off at the top and bottom of each unit as shown.

3. The diagrams show how the Rectrangle should look at top and bottom when 1/4" is trimmed off. The dashed lines on the right diagrams show your seam allowance, and the measurement at the top gives you the size after trimming off the top and bottom. Make 7 of each Rectrangle. For more on making Rectrangles, refer to page 8.

4. To assemble the place mat, join units 1 and 2 as shown. Make 7. Join the seven rows of "Goony Birds" together, carefully matching seams. Join Unit Q3 to opposite sides of the Goony Bird row. Join Unit Q4 and remaining Unit Q3 as shown. Join these combined units to the right side of the Goony Birds. Join Unit Q5 to top and bottom of place mat to complete it.

Quilting and Finishing

1. Mary used a mixture of matching thread and gold metallic thread to quilt this place mat. She quilted a beautiful feather design in the medium teal space, and quilted swirls with gold metallic thread in the green spaces. The patchwork was "ditched."

2. Use two 2 1/2" wide strips of Fabric I to bind your place mat. Refer to page 13 for French-fold binding.

CUTTING FOR HALF STAR PLACE MAT

■ **FROM FABRIC I, CUT: (DARK TEAL PRINT)**
- **Three 2 1/2" wide strips. Two for straight-grain binding.**
  From remaining strip, cut:
  * Four - 2 1/2" x 5" (1a, 2a)
- **Two 1 1/2" wide strips. From these, cut:**
  * Two - 1 1/2" x 20 1/2" (9)
  * Two - 1 1/2" x 14 1/2" (8)

■ **FROM FABRIC II, CUT: (MEDIUM TEAL PRINT)**
- **One 4 1/2" wide strip. From this, cut:**
  * Two - 4 1/2" squares (4)
  * One - 2 1/2" x 4 1/2" (3)

■ **FROM FABRIC III, CUT: (MEDIUM GREEN BATIK)**
- **One 9 1/2" wide strip. From this, cut:**
  * One - 9 1/2" x 12 1/2" (6)
  * Four - 2 1/2" x 5" (1, 2)
  * Two - 2 1/2" squares (3a)

■ **FROM FABRIC IV, CUT: (PALE GREEN PRINT)**
- **One 3" wide strip. From these, cut:**
  * Four - 3" squares (4a, 6a)
  Stack this cut:
  * Two - 1 1/2" x 18 1/2" (7)
- **One 1 1/2" wide strip. From this, cut:**
  * Three - 1 1/2" x 12 1/2" (5)

Half Star Place Mat Assembly

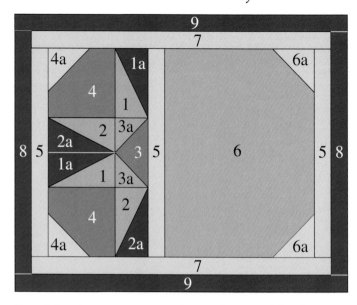

For this place mat you will need: 10 1/2" of Fabric I, 4 1/2" of Fabric II, 9 1/2" of Fabric III, and 4 1/2" of Fabric IV. Need 20 1/2" x 24 1/2" for backing.

1. For the Rectrangles, draw a line diagonally from one corner to the other. Place rectangles as shown in diagrams below. Pin if necessary so that the Rectrangles do not slip.

2. Press the top Rectrangle over as shown. Trim top Rectrangles even with foundation unit if necessary. Trim 1/4" off at the top and bottom of each unit as shown.

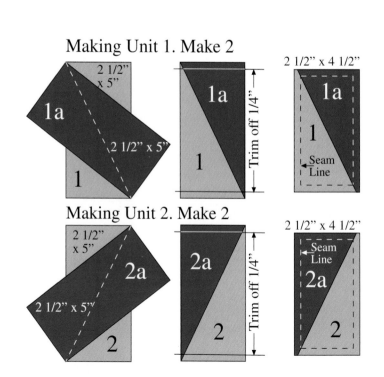

Half Star Place Mat Assembly Continued

3. The diagrams show how the Rectrangle should look at top and bottom when 1/4" is trimmed off. The dashed lines on the right diagrams show your seam allowance, and the measurement at the top gives you the size after trimming off the top and bottom. Make 2 of each Rectrangle. For more on making Rectrangles, refer to page 8.

4. Use diagonal corner technique to make two of Unit 4, and one each of units 3 and 6.

5. To piece the place mat, beginning in the top left corner of the star design, join units 4 and 1 as shown. Join units 1 and 2; then add Unit 3 to right side of the 1-2 combined units, matching points. Join units 4 and 2 as shown. Join these three sections together, again carefully matching seams. Join Unit 5 to opposite sides of the half star. Join the remaining Unit 5 to the right side of Unit 6; then add these combined units to the right side of the half star section. Join Unit 7 to the top and bottom. Join Unit 8 to opposite sides of the place mat; then join Unit 9 to the top and bottom to complete the place mat top.

Quilting and Finishing

1. Mary used a mixture of matching thread and gold metallic thread to quilt this place mat. She stippled the medium teal areas behind the star, and quilted a feather swirl design in the large green batik area. A circular design with swirls was quilted in the pale green border, and accents were quilted on the star points with gold metallic thread.

2. Use two 2 1/2" wide strips of Fabric I to bind your place mat. Refer to page 13 for French-fold binding.

CUTTING FOR CAT'S EYE PLACE MAT

FROM FABRIC I, CUT: (DARK TEAL PRINT)
- **One 12 1/2" wide strip. From this, cut:**
  * One - 10 1/2" x 12 1/2" (B1)
  Stack these cuts:
  * Two - 2 1/2" x 6 1/2" (B6)
  * Twelve - 2 1/2" x 3 1/2" (A6, A7, A8, A9, B5, B7)
  * Two - 1 1/2" x 4 1/2" (B4)
  * Sixteen - 1 1/2" x 3" (A2a, A3a, A4a, A5a, B2a, B3a)
- **Three 2 1/2" wide strips. Two for straight-grain binding. From remaining strip, cut:**
  * Eight - 2 1/2" squares (A1a)

FROM FABRIC II, CUT: (MEDIUM TEAL PRINT)
- **One 2 1/2" wide strip. From this, cut:**
  * Four - 2 1/2" squares (A7a, A9a)
  * Four - 1 1/2" x 3" (A4, A5)

FROM FABRIC III, CUT: (LIGHT GREEN BATIK)
- **One 2 1/2" wide strip. From this, cut:**
  * Eight - 2 1/2" squares (A6a, A8a, B5a, B7a)
- **One 1 1/2" wide strip. From this, cut:**
  * Twelve - 1 1/2" x 3" (A2, A3, B2, B3)

FROM FABRIC IV, CUT: (PALE GREEN PRINT)
- **One 4 1/2" wide strip. From this, cut:**
  * Two - 4 1/2" squares (A1)
  * Two - 1 1/2" x 16 1/2" (Unit 8)

Cat's Eye Place Mat Assembly

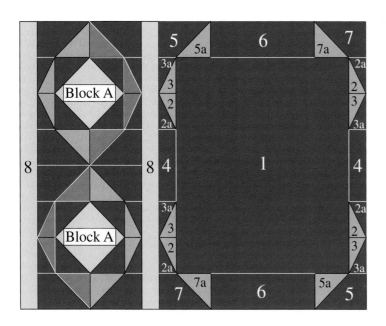

For this place mat you will need: 20" of Fabric I, 2 1/2" of Fabric II, 4" of Fabric III, and 4 1/2" of Fabric IV. Need 20 1/2" x 24 1/2" for backing.

Block A Assembly

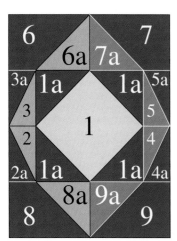

Block A, Make 2. When completed, block should measure 6 1/2" x 8 1/2".

1. For the Rectrangles, draw a line diagonally from one corner to the other. Place rectrangles as shown in diagrams at right. Pin if necessary so that the Rectrangles do not slip.

2. Press the top Rectrangle over as shown. Trim top Rectrangles even with foundation unit if necessary. Trim 1/4" off at the top and bottom of each unit as shown.

3. The diagrams show how the Rectrangle should look at top and bottom when 1/4" is trimmed off. The dashed lines on the right diagrams show your seam allowance, and the measurement at the top gives you the size after trimming off the top and bottom. Make the required number of each Rectrangle. For more on making Rectrangles, refer to page 8.

4. Use diagonal corner technique to make one of units 1, 6, 7, 8, and 9.

Making units A2 and B2. Make 6.

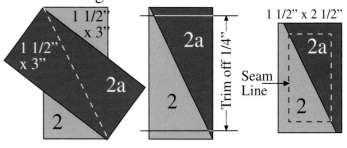

Making units A3 and B3. Make 6.

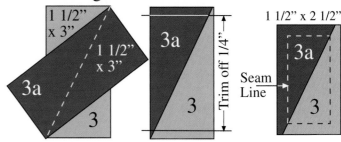

Making Unit A4. Make 2

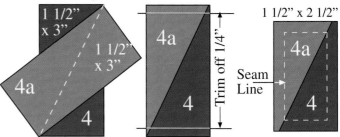

Making Unit A5. Make 2

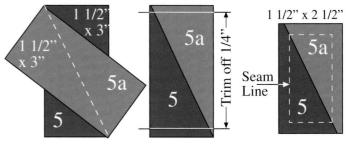

Block A Assembly Continued

5. To assemble Block A, begin by joining units 6 and 7. Join units 3 and 2 as shown, matching points. Join units 5 and 4 together, again matching points. Join the 2-3 combined units to the left side of Unit 1, and the 5-4 combined units to the right side of Unit 1, carefully matching the point seams. Join units 8 and 9.

6. Join the combined 6-7 units to the top of the center "eye" section, and the combined 8-9 units to the bottom. Match the center points to complete the block. Make 2.

Block B Assembly

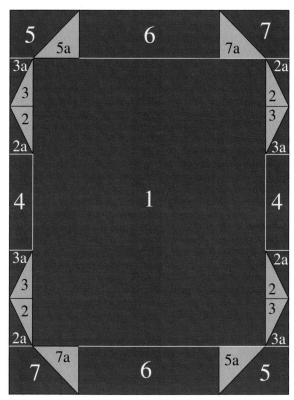

Block B. Make 1. When completed block should measure 12 1/2" x 16 1/2"

1. Use diagonal corner technique to make two each of mirror image units 5 and 7.

2. Refer to the instructions and diagrams on page 106 for the Rectrangles.

3. To assemble Block B, begin by joining units 5, 6, and 7 in a horizontal row. For the left side of the block, refer to the diagram for correct position of all units and join units 3, 2, 4, 3, and 2. Join to the left side of Unit 1 as shown. For the right side of the block, join units 2, 3, 4,

2, and 3 in a vertical row. Join this row to the right side of Unit 1. Join units 7, 6, and 5. Join previously pieced units 5-6-7 to the top of the block; then add the 7-6-5 combined units to the bottom to complete the block. Make 1.

Cat's Eye Place Mat Assembly

1. Join the two Block A's together as shown in the place mat diagram on page 106. Join Unit 8 to opposite sides of the combined Block A's. Join Block B to the right side of the Cat's Eye combined blocks to complete the place mat.

Quilting and Finishing

1. Again Mary used a mixture of matching thread and gold metallic thread to quilt this place mat. With gold metallic thread, she worked a small feather design in the center of the Cat's Eye, and on the pale green strips. A larger feather design was worked in the dark teal open area with darker thread, and the patchwork was "ditched."

2. Use two 2 1/2" wide strips of Fabric I to bind your place mat. Refer to page 13 for French-fold binding.

Stars at Sea

With large Rectrangles and strip sets, this is easy piecing and makes an attractive lap quilt or wall hanging. Choosing similar colors gives it a masculine look, making it perfect for that special man's den or office.

Wall quilt finishes to: 54" square.
Techniques used: Rectrangles, and strip sets.

MATERIALS FOR QUILT

Fabric I (navy print)
Need 72 1/2"   2 1/8 yards

Fabric II (medium blue print)
Need 27 1/2"   7/8 yard

Fabric III (pale blue print)
Need 15"   1/2 yard

Fabric IV (ivory print)
Need 22 1/2"   3/4 yard

Fabric V (dark rust print)
Need 7 1/2"   3/8 yard

Fabric VI (light rust print)
Need 5"   1/4 yard

Fabric VII (honey tan print)
Need 27 1/2"   7/8 yard

Backing   **3 1/4 yards**

CUTTING FOR QUILT

▪ FROM FABRIC I, CUT: (NAVY PRINT)
- **Four 5" wide strips. From these, cut:**
  - * Sixty-four - 2 1/2" x 5" (A5, A7, A9, A12, A14, A15, A18, A19)
- **Twenty-one 2 1/2" wide strips. Six for straight-grain binding, and seven for strip sets 1, 2, 3 and 4. From remainder, cut:**
  - * Four - 2 1/2" x 27 1/4" (Q4) Piece two together to = two 54" lengths.
  - * Four - 2 1/2" x 25 1/4" (Q3) Piece two together to = two 50" lengths.
  - * Twenty-four - 2 1/2" sq. (A3)

▪ FROM FABRIC II, CUT: (MEDIUM BLUE PRINT)
- **Four 5" wide strips. From these, cut:**
  - * Sixty-four - 2 1/2" x 5" (A6, A8, A10, A11, A13, A16, A17, A20)
- **Three 2 1/2" wide strips for Strip Set 4.**

▫ FROM FABRIC III, CUT: (PALE BLUE PRINT)
- **Three 5" wide strips. From these, cut:**
  - * Forty-eight - 2 1/2" x 5" (A9a, A10a, A11a, A12a, A14a, A16a, A17a, A19a)

▫ FROM FABRIC IV, CUT: (IVORY PRINT)
- **One 5" wide strips. From this, cut:**
  - * Sixteen - 2 1/2" x 5" (A13a, A15a, A18a, A20a)
- **Three 2 1/2" wide strips. Two for strip sets 3 and 5. From remainder, cut:**
  - * Eight - 2 1/2" x 4 1/2" (A2)
- **Eight 1 1/4" wide strips. From these, cut:**
  - * Four - 1 1/4" x 25 1/4" (Q2) Piece two together to = two 50" lengths.
  - * Four - 1 1/4" x 24 1/2" (Q1) Piece two together to = two 48 1/2" lengths.

▪ FROM FABRIC V, CUT: (DARK RUST PRINT)
- **Three 2 1/2" wide strips for strip sets 2 and 6.**

▪ FROM FABRIC VI, CUT: (LIGHT RUST PRINT)
- **Two 2 1/2" wide strips. One for Strip Set 5. From remainder, cut:**
  - * Eight - 2 1/2" squares (A4)

▪ FROM FABRIC VII, CUT: (HONEY TAN PRINT)
- **Four 5" wide strips. From these, cut:**
  - * Sixty-four - 2 1/2" x 5" (A5a, A6a, A7a, A8a)
- **Three 2 1/2" wide strips. Two for strip sets 1 and 6. From remainder, cut:**
  - * Eight - 2 1/2" x 4 1/2" (A1)

Strip Sets For Block A

Strip Set 1. Make 1
Cut into sixteen
2 1/2" segments

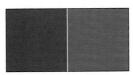

Strip Set 2. Make 2
Cut into twenty-four
2 1/2" segments

Strip Set 3. Make 1
Cut into sixteen
2 1/2" segments

Strip Set 4. Make 3.
Cut into forty
2 1/2" segments

Strip Set 5. Make 1.
Cut into eight
4 1/2" segments

Strip Set 6. Make 1.
Cut into eight
4 1/2" segments

See page 6 for making Strip Sets. Join the strip sets shown above as directed, and cut into the required number of segments.

Block A Assembly

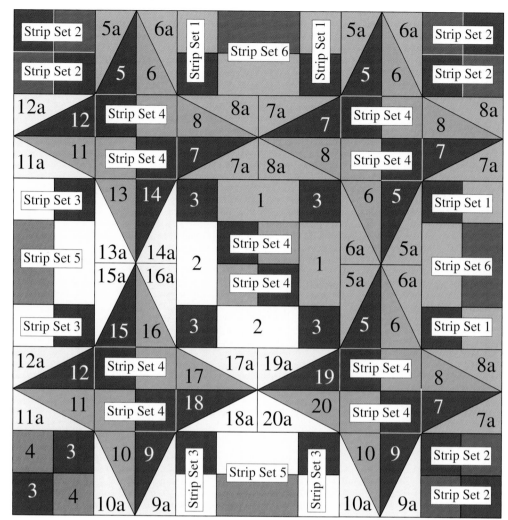

Block A. Make 4. When completed, block should measure 24 1/2" square.

Rectrangles For Block A

1. For the Rectrangles on pages 112 and 113, draw a line diagonally from one corner to the other. Place Rectrangles as shown in diagrams at right. Pin if necessary so that the Rectrangles do not slip.

2. Press the top Rectrangle over as shown. Trim top Rectrangles even with foundation unit if necessary. Trim 1/4" off at the top and bottom of each unit as shown.

3. The diagrams show how the Rectrangle should look at top and bottom when 1/4" is trimmed off. The dashed lines on the third diagrams show your seam allowance, and the measurement at the top gives you the size after trimming off the top and bottom. Make the required number of each Rectrangle shown. For more on making Rectrangles, refer to page 8.

Making Unit 5. Make 16.

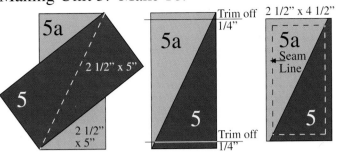

Making Unit 20. Make 4.

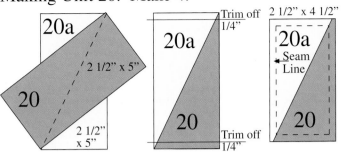

Making Unit 8. Make 16.

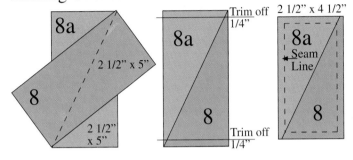

Making units 9 and 14. Make 8 of Unit 9. Make 4 of Unit 14.

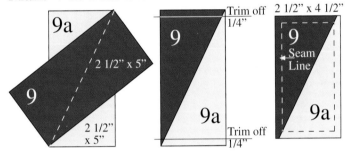

Making Unit 6. Make 16.

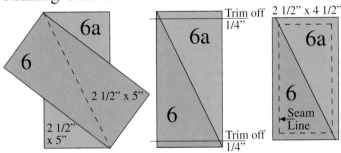

Making Unit 7. Make 16.

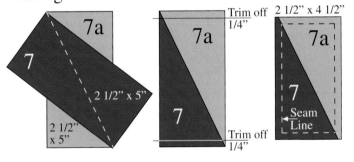

Making units 11 and 17. Make 8. of Unit 11, and 4 of Unit 17.

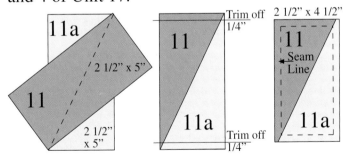

Making units 10 and 16. Make 8 of Unit 10. Make 4 of Unit 16.

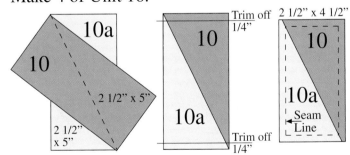

Making Unit 15. Make 4.

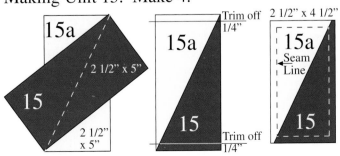

112

Making units 12 and 19. Make 8 of Unit 12. Make 4 of Unit 19.

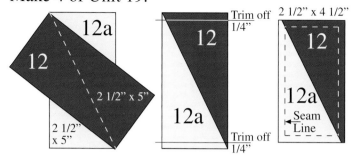

Making Unit 13. Make 4.

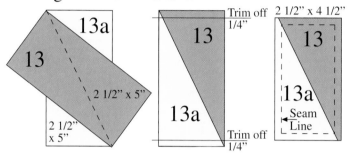

Making Unit 18. Make 4.

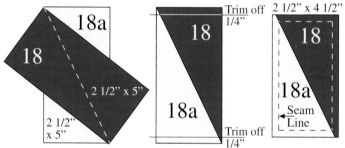

Block A Assembly Continued

1. Refer to the block diagram on page 111 frequently for correct position of all units. These instructions are for one of Block A. The block will be pieced in three sections: the left side section, center section, and right side section.

2. Beginning with the left side, in the top left corner, join two of Strip Set 2, matching seams as shown. Make a total of three. Working down the row, join units 12 and 11. Make two. Join one pair to the bottom of the combined Strip Set 2 units. Join strip sets 3, 5, and 3; then add the previously pieced 12-11 combined units to the bottom of Strip Set 3. Join these combined units to the bottom of Unit 11 as shown. Join units 4 And 3. Make 2 and join them together, matching seams. Join these combined units to the bottom of Unit 11 to complete the vertical row.

3. For the second row on the left, join units 5 and 6. Make 4. Join two of Strip Set 4 together, matching seams. Make 5. Add the combined strip sets to the bottom of combined 5-6 units, carefully matching seams. Join units 13 and 14. Join units 15 and 16; then join these two combined units together, matching the points. Join these combined units to the bottom of previously pieced Strip Set 4 units as shown, again matching seams. Join units 10 and 9; then add these combined units to the bottom of the previously pieced Strip Set 4 units. Join these combined units to the bottom of combined units 15-16, matching seams, to complete the row. Join the two rows together, pinning where seams need to match to complete the left side of the block.

4. For the center section, join Strip Set 1 to opposite sides of Strip Set 6 as shown. Refer to the block diagram for correct placement and join units 7 and 8. Make 2. Join these combined star units together as shown, carefully matching points. Add them to the bottom of the combined strip set units. Join Unit 1 to the top of previously pieced Strip Set 4 combined units; then join Unit 2 to the bottom. Join Unit 3 to top and bottom of Unit 2. Join Unit 3 to top and bottom of Unit 1 as shown. Join the 3-2-3 units to the left side of the center section, and the 3-1-3 combined units to the right side, matching seams. Join this center section to the bottom of the other combined units. Join units 17 and 18. Join units 19 and 20; then join them together as shown, matching the points. Join these combined units to the bottom of the other combined units. To complete the row, join Strip Set 3 to opposite sides of Strip Set 5, matching seams. Join these combined strip set units to the bottom of combined units 17-20 to complete the center row. Join the center section to the left side section as shown, again matching all seams.

5. For the first row on the right, join previously pieced combined units 5-6 to combined strip sets 4. Join two of the 5-6 combined units together as shown, carefully matching the points. Join these combined units to the bottom of the combined Strip Set 4's; then add the remaining combined Strip Set 4's to the bottom of the other combined units. Join units 9 and 10; then join these units to the bottom of combined Strip Set 4 units to complete the row.

6. For the final row on the right, join units 8 and 7 as shown. Make 2. Join previously pieced Strip Set 2 combination to the top of the combined 8-7 units. Join strip sets 1, 6, and 1 in a vertical row as shown. Add this row to the bottom of Unit 7. Join the remaining previously pieced Strip Set 2's to the bottom of combined 8-7 units; then add these combined units to the bottom of Strip Set 1 to complete the row. Join the two right side rows together, pinning where seams need to be matched. Join the right side of the block to the center section, again carefully matching seams to complete the block. Make 4.

Quilt Assembly And Finishing

1. Join the four Block A's together as shown, turning them so that the lightest section is in the center, match all seams and star points. Join Unit Q1 to opposite sides of the quilt; then add Unit Q2 to the top and bottom. Join border Q3 to opposite sides of the quilt; then join Unit Q4 to the top to complete the quilt top.

2. We suggest "ditching" the patchwork for quilting. Join the six 2 1/2" wide strips of Fabric I together, and refer to page 13 for straight-grain binding.

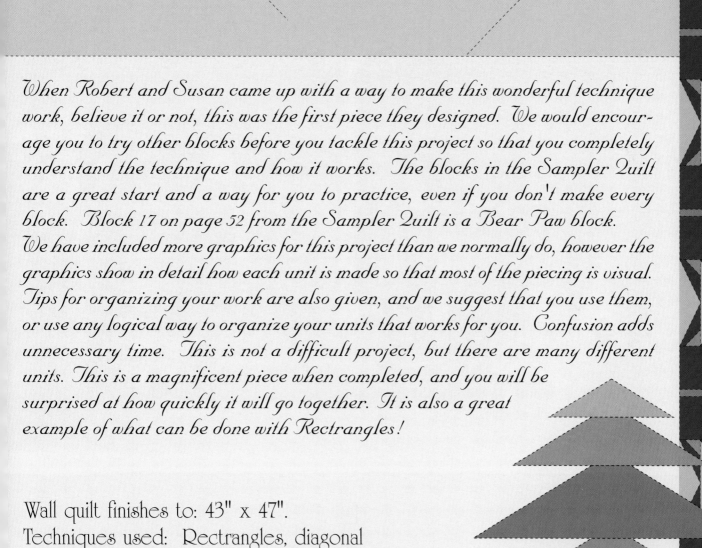

When Robert and Susan came up with a way to make this wonderful technique work, believe it or not, this was the first piece they designed. We would encourage you to try other blocks before you tackle this project so that you completely understand the technique and how it works. The blocks in the Sampler Quilt are a great start and a way for you to practice, even if you don't make every block. Block 17 on page 52 from the Sampler Quilt is a Bear Paw block. We have included more graphics for this project than we normally do, however the graphics show in detail how each unit is made so that most of the piecing is visual. Tips for organizing your work are also given, and we suggest that you use them, or use any logical way to organize your units that works for you. Confusion adds unnecessary time. This is not a difficult project, but there are many different units. This is a magnificent piece when completed, and you will be surprised at how quickly it will go together. It is also a great example of what can be done with Rectrangles!

Wall quilt finishes to: 43" x 47".
Techniques used: Rectrangles, diagonal corners, Rectrangles with diagonal corners, and Rectrangles used as diagnal corners.

KODIAK

MATERIALS FOR KODIAK

Fabric I (pale olive print)
Need 22"   3/4 yard

Fabric II (medium green batik swirl)
Need 2"   1/8 yard

Fabric III (medium green batik)
Need 7 1/4"   3/8 yard

Fabric IV (dark green batik)
Need 8 5/8"   3/8 yard

Fabric V (medium lavender print)
Need 14 1/4"   1/2 yard

Fabric VI (light blue textured print)
Need 10 1/2"   3/8 yard

Fabric VII (medium blue print)
Need 32 1/2"   1 1/8 yards

Fabric VIII (dark blue textured print)
Need 14"   1/2 yard

Fabric IX (dark brown batik)
Need 17"   5/8 yard

Fabric X (medium brown batik)
Need 3 3/4"   1/4 yard

Fabric XI (honey tan batik)
Need 3 1/4"   1/4 yard

Fabric XII (white on white print)
Need 4 3/4"   1/4 yard
Backing   **3 1/2 yards**

CUTTING FOR KODIAK

FROM FABRIC I, CUT: (PALE OLIVE PRINT)
- **One 9" wide strip. From this, cut:**
  - One - 5 1/2" x 9" (49)
  - One - 5 1/2" x 8 1/2" (48)
  - One - 2" x 8 1/2" (42)
  - One - 2 1/2" x 8" (32)
  - One - 2 1/4" x 8" (22)
  - Two - 1 7/8" x 7 7/8" (9)
  - One - 2" x 7 3/4" (43)
  - One - 3 1/2" x 7 1/2" (36)
  - Two - 2 1/2" x 7 1/2" (33, 39)
  - Two - 3 1/8" x 7" (5)
  - One - 1" x 5 3/4" (21)
- **One 7" wide strip. From this, cut:**
  - Two - 6 1/8" x 7" (2)
  - Three - 3 1/2" x 7" (38, 46)
  - Four - 2 1/4" x 7" (3, 7)
  - One - 1" x 4 3/4" (31)
  - One - 3 1/4" x 4 1/4" (14)
  - One - 1 1/2" x 4 1/4" (19)
  - One - 1 1/2" x 3 3/4" (30)
- **One 3 1/2" wide strip. From this, cut:**
  - One - 1 3/4" x 3 1/2" (16)
  - One - 3 3/8" x 14 3/4" (10)
  - One - 2 1/2" x 3" (24)
  - Two - 1 1/2" x 3" (28a)
  - One - 1" x 2 3/4" (12)
  - One - 2" square (18a)
- **One 2 1/2" wide strip. From this, cut:**
  - Four - 2 1/2" x 6 3/4" (35, 41, 44)

FROM FABRIC II, CUT: (MEDIUM GREEN BATIK SWIRL)
- **One 2" wide strip. From this, cut:**
  - Four - 2" x 4" (42a, 43a, 52a)
  - Two - 1 7/8" x 3 3/4" (9a)

FROM FABRIC III, CUT: (MEDIUM GREEN BATIK)
- **One 5" wide strip. From this, cut:**
  - Eight - 2 1/2" x 5" (33a, 35a, 39a, 41a, 44a, 51a)
  - Four - 2 1/4" x 4 1/2" (3a, 7a)
  - Two - 2 1/2" squares (40, 50)
  - Four - 1 1/2" x 2 1/2" (34, 45)
- **One 2 1/4" wide strip. From this, cut:**
  - One - 2 1/4" square (8)
  - Two - 1 3/8" x 2 1/4" (4)

FROM FABRIC IV, CUT: (DARK GREEN BATIK)
- **One 3 1/2" wide strip. From this, cut:**
  - Four - 3 1/2" x 7" (36a, 38a, 46a)
  - Two - 2 1/2" x 3 1/2" (37, 47)
- **One 3 1/8" wide strip. From this, cut:**
  - Two - 3 1/8" x 6 1/4" (5a)
  - One - 2 1/4" x 3 1/8" (6)
- **One 2" wide strip. From this, cut:**
  - One - 2" x 31" (70)

FROM FABRIC V, CUT: (MEDIUM LAVENDER BATIK)
- **One 5 3/4" wide strip. From this, cut:**
  - Two - 2" x 5 3/4" (52)
  - Two - 5 1/2" x 11" (62, 68)
  - One - 5 1/2" square (62c)
  - One - 5" x 5 1/2" (65)
- **One 5 1/2" wide strip. From this, cut:**
  - Two - 2 3/4" x 5 1/2" (64)
  - Two - 2 1/2" x 5" (51)
  - One - 4 1/2" x 10 1/2" (67)
  - One - 4" x 7" (55)
  - Two - 3 1/2" x 7" (57a, 58a)
  - One - 2" x 4" (54)
- **One 3" wide strip. From this, cut:**
  - One - 3" x 9" (60)
  - One - 3" x 6 1/2" (59)
  - One - 1" x 4" (53)

FROM FABRIC VI, CUT: (LIGHT BLUE TEXTURED PRINT)
- **One 6" wide strip. From this, cut:**
  - One - 6" square (61)
  - Two - 5 1/2" x 11" (62b, 68b)
  - Two - 2 3/4" x 5 1/2" (64b)
  - One - 2 1/2" x 5 1/2" (63)
  - One - 3" x 5" (66)
- **One 4 1/2" wide strip. From this, cut:**
  - One - 4 1/2" square (67b)
  - One - 4" square (55b)
  - One - 2 1/2" x 4" (56)
  - One - 3 1/2" x 7" (58b)
  - One - 2 1/2" x 9 1/2" (69)

FROM FABRIC VII, CUT: (MEDIUM BLUE PRINT)
- **Four 3 1/2" wide strips. From these, cut:**
  - Two - 3 1/2" x 22" (76)
  - Two - 3 1/2" x 18" (73)
  - Twelve - 3 1/2" squares (A2, B2, C2)
  - Eight - 1" x 3 1/2" (71)
  - Six - 2" x 4" (A1, B1, C1, C4)

- Five 2 1/2” wide strips for straight-grain binding.
- Three 2” wide strips. From these, cut:
  * Twenty-six - 2” x 4” (add to 2” x 4” above)

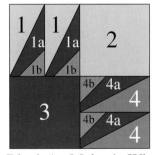 FROM FABRIC VIII, CUT: (DARK BLUE TEXTURED PRINT)
- Four 3 1/2” wide strips. From these, cut:
  * Two - 3 1/2” x 22” (75)
  * Two - 3 1/2” x 18” (74)
  * Eight - 1” x 3 1/2” (72)
  * Sixteen - 2” x 4” (A4, B4)

FROM FABRIC IX, CUT: (DARK BROWN BATIK)
- Two 3 1/2” wide strips. From these, cut:
  * Twelve - 3 1/2” squares (A3, B3, C3)
  * One - 2” x 16 1/2” (11)
  * One - 2” x 8” (23)
  * One - 1 3/4” x 6 1/8” (1)
  From scrap, cut:
  * Four - 1 1/4” squares (34a, 45a)
  * Two - 1 1/8” squares (4a)
- Five 2” wide strips. From these, cut:
  * Forty-eight - 2” x 4” (A1a, A4a, B1a, B4a, C1a, C4a)

FROM FABRIC X, CUT: (MEDIUM BROWN BATIK)
- One 3 3/4” wide strip. From this, cut:
  * One - 2 3/4” x 3 3/4” (27)
  * One - 1 3/4” x 3 3/4” (26)
  * One - 1 3/4” x 3 1/2” (16a)
  * One - 1 3/4” x 3” (25)
  * Two - 1 1/2” x 3” (19a, 30a)
  * One - 1 1/4” x 3” (15)
  * One - 2 3/4” x 5 3/4” (18)
  * One - 1 3/4” x 2 1/2” (17)
  * One - 1 1/2” x 2 1/4” (20)
  * One - 2” square (14a)
  * One - 1” x 2” (13)
  * One - 1 3/4” square (14b)
  * One - 1 1/2” x 7” (28)
  * One - 1 1/2” x 1 3/4” (29)
  * Three - 1 1/4” squares (14c, 24a)

FROM FABRIC XI, CUT: (HONEY TAN BATIK)
- Two 1 5/8” wide strips. From these, cut:
  * Forty-eight - 1 5/8” squares (A1b, A4b, B1b, B4b, C1b, C4b)

☐ FROM FABRIC XII, CUT: (WHITE ON WHITE PRINT)
- One 4 3/4” wide strip. From this, cut:
  * One - 4 3/4” square (68a)
  * One - 4 1/2” square (67a)
  * One - 4 1/4” square (62a)
  * One - 4” square (55a)
  * Two - 3 1/2” x 7” (57, 58)
  * Two - 2 3/4” squares (64a)

ORGANIZING YOUR WORK FOR THIS PROJECT.

1. Although the project is not difficult, with most of the matching up in the bear, and mountains, there are many units. Label the units with a piece of masking tape as you cut them, *and* as you piece them.
2. If you are joining multiple units, label them as well as you complete them. This insures that you can find the completed units when it is time to assemble the block. It is also useful to put like colors together, such as the pale olive background units, and the lavender mountain units.
3. Follow our step-by-step instructions, as the units are in numerical order and with the additional graphics, you will be assembling the units in the order given.

ASSEMBLY FOR BLOCKS A, B, AND C.

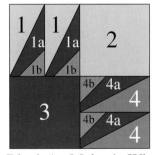

Block A. Make 4. When completed, block should measure, 6 1/2”square.

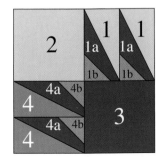

Block B. Make 4. When completed, block should measure, 6 1/2”square.

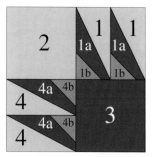

Block C. Make 4. When completed, block should measure, 6 1/2" square.

ABOUT THE RECTRANGLES.

1. For the Rectrangles, draw a line diagonally from one corner to the other. Place Rectrangles as shown in diagrams. Pin if necessary so that the Rectrangles do not slip.

2. Press the top Rectrangle over as shown on all Rectrangle diagrams. Trim top Rectrangles even with foundation unit if necessary. Trim 1/4" off at the top and bottom of each unit as shown in the individual diagrams. Some diagrams and instructions may only require that you trim off the top or bottom. These are Rectrangle Diagonal Corners.

3. The diagrams show how the Rectrangle should look at top and bottom when 1/4" is trimmed off. In the case of the Rectrangles on the right, the diagonal corner is joined after trimming the unit as shown. The dashed lines on the last diagrams show your seam allowance, and the measurement at the top gives you the size after trimming off the top and/or bottom. For more on making Rectrangles, refer to page 8. Make the required number of units shown with each diagram, and label them.

ASSEMBLING THE BLOCKS

1. For Block A, Join two of Unit A1 as shown; then add Unit A2 to the right side of the combined A1 units. Join two of Unit A4; then add Unit A3 to the left side of the combined Unit A4's. Join the top and bottom together to complete the block. Make 4.

2. Blocks B and C are the same, except for the color of Unit 4. Refer to the block diagrams for the correct colors. Join two of Unit 1 as shown; then add Unit 2 to the left side of the combined 1 units. Join two of Unit 4; then add Unit 3 to the right side of the combined Unit 4's. Join the two sections together to complete the blocks. Make 4 of blocks B and C. Set aside.

Making mirror image Bear Paw block units 1 and 4.

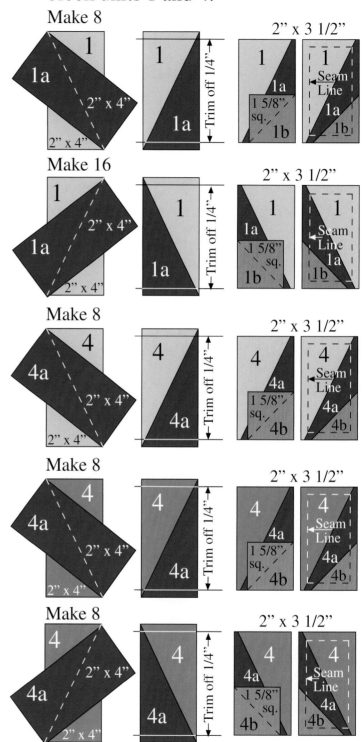

MAKING THE INDIVIDUAL UNITS

1. Use diagonal corner technique to complete the following units: two of mirror image units 4, 34, and 45 one each of units 14, 18, 24, 55, and 67. Please note that units 55 and 67 have double diagonal corners. Join these corners in alphabetical order. Other diagonal corners on Rectrangles are included with the graphics of those units.

2. Refer to the Rectrangle diagrams and instructions with each diagram to make the units. Label each unit after it is completed.

Making mirror image units 3 & 7.

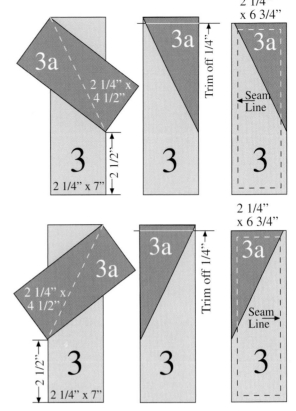

Mirror image units 3 and 7 are made the same way, and are the same size. Make one of each mirror image for units 3 and 7.

Making mirror image Unit 9.
Make 1 of each.

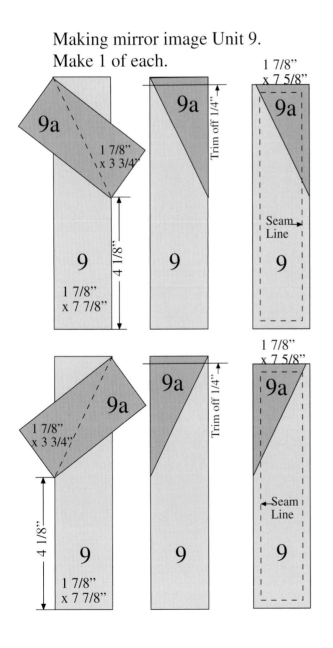

Making mirror image Unit 5.
Make 1 of each.

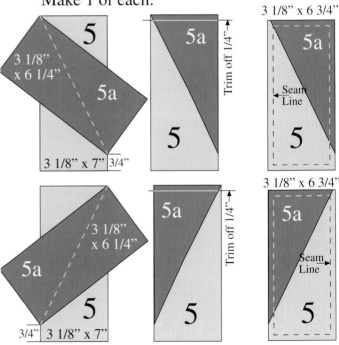

120

Making Unit 16. Make 1.

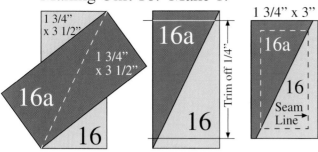

1 3/4" x 3 1/2"
1 3/4" x 3 1/2"
1 3/4" x 3"
Trim off 1/4"
Seam Line

Making Unit 30. Make 1.

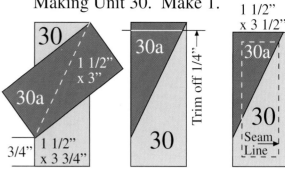

1 1/2" x 3 1/2"
1 1/2" x 3"
3/4"
1 1/2" x 3 3/4"
Trim off 1/4"
Seam Line

Making Unit 19. Make 1.

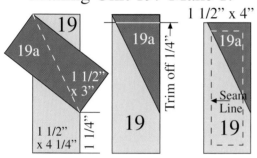

1 1/2" x 3"
1 1/2" x 4 1/4"
1 1/4"
1 1/2" x 4"
Trim off 1/4"
Seam Line

Making Units 33 & 39. Make 2. One for Unit 33, and one for Unit 39.

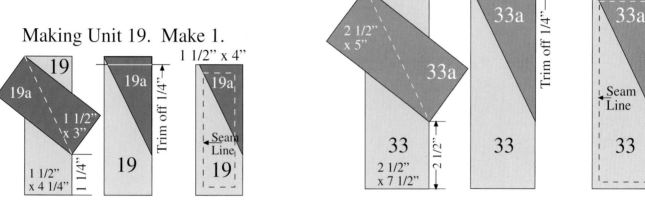

2 1/2" x 5"
2 1/2" x 7 1/2"
2 1/2"
2 1/2" x 7 1/4"
Trim off 1/4"
Seam Line

Making Unit 36. Make 1.

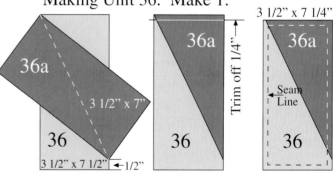

3 1/2" x 7"
3 1/2" x 7 1/2"
1/2"
3 1/2" x 7 1/4"
Trim off 1/4"
Seam Line

Making Unit 28 Make 1.

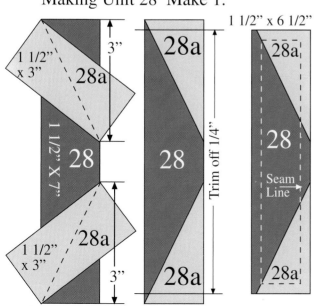

1 1/2" x 3"
1 1/2" X 7"
1 1/2" x 3"
3"
3"
Trim off 1/4"
Seam Line
1 1/2" x 6 1/2"

Making Unit 38. Make 1.

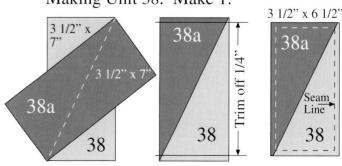

3 1/2" x 7"
3 1/2" x 7"
3 1/2" x 6 1/2"
Trim off 1/4"
Seam Line

Making Units 35 & 41. Make 2. One for Unit 35, and one for Unit 41.

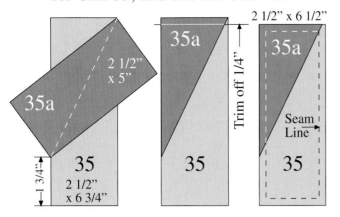

Making mirror image Unit 44. Make 1 of each.

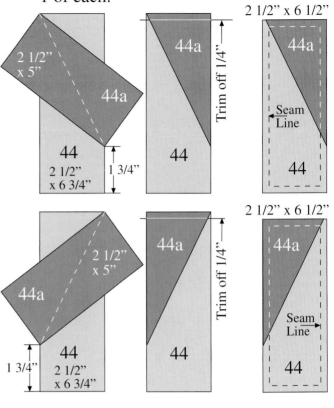

Making Unit 42. Make 1.

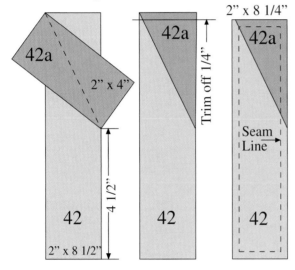

Making Unit 43. Make 1.

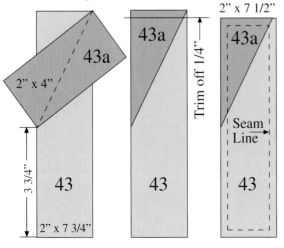

Making mirror image Unit 46. Make 1 of each.

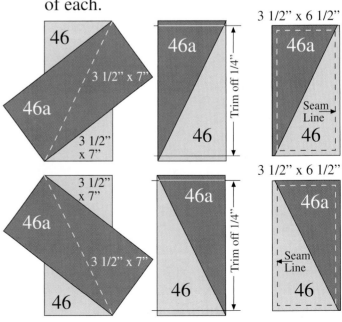

Making mirror image Unit 51. Make 1 of each.

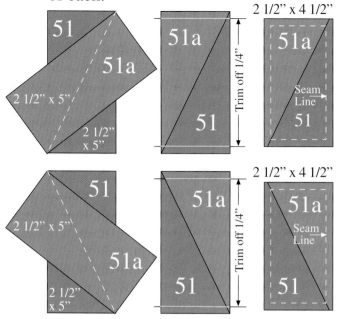

Making mirror image Unit 52. Make 1 of each.

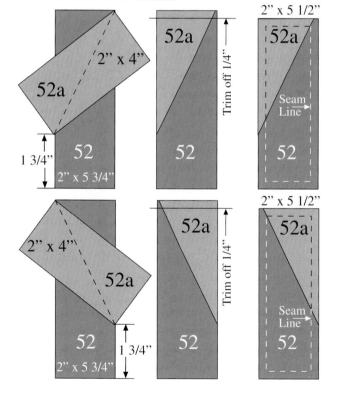

Making Unit 57. Make 1.

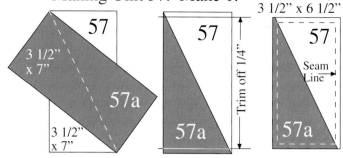

Making Unit 58. Make 1.

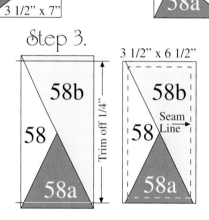

Step 1. Join Rectrangles as shown. Press.
Step 2. Join Rectrangle, Unit 58b as shown. Press.
Step 3. Trim off 1/4" from top and bottom of unit.
Completed unit should measure 3 1/2" x 6 1/2".

Making Combined Units 57-61.

Step 1.

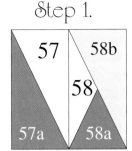

Step 2.   Step 3.

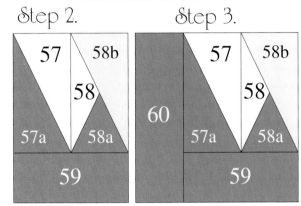

Step 4.

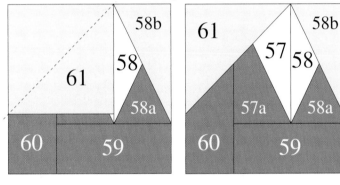

Step 1. Join units 57 and 58, matching points.
Step 2. Join Unit 59 to the bottom of combined units 57-58.
Step 3. Join Unit 60 to the left side of the combined units as shown.
Step 4. Join diagonal corner, Unit 61 with right sides facing and raw edges matching. Press.

Making Unit 62. Make 1.

Step 1.   Step 2.

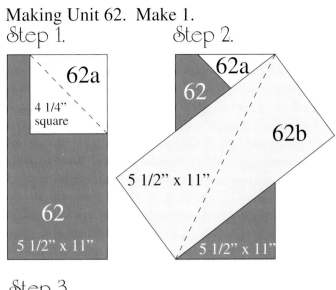

Step 3.

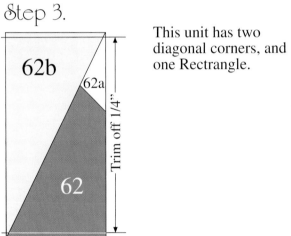

This unit has two diagonal corners, and one Rectrangle.

Step 4.

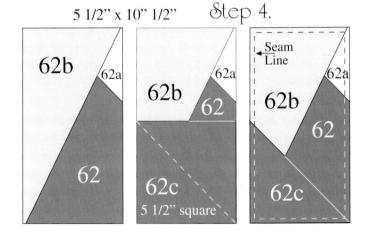

Step 1. Join diagonal corner 62a as shown. DO NOT trim seam as the darker fabric behind 62a will show through. Press.
Step 2. Join the Rectrangle as shown. Press and trim.
Step 3. Trim off 1/4" from top and bottom of unit.
Step 4. Unit should measure 5 1/2" x 10 1/2" after trimming. Join diagonal corner 62c as shown. Trim seam and press.

Making mirror image Unit 64. Make 1 of each.

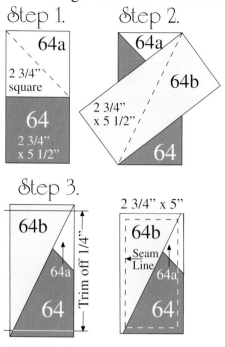

Step 1.

64a
2 3/4" square
64
2 3/4" x 5 1/2"

Step 2.

64a
64b
2 3/4" x 5 1/2"
64

Step 3.

64b
64a
64
Trim off 1/4"

2 3/4" x 5"
64b
Seam Line
64a
64

Mirror image Unit 64.

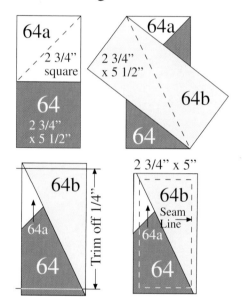

64a
2 3/4" square
64
2 3/4" x 5 1/2"

64a
2 3/4" x 5 1/2"
64b
64

64b
64a
64
Trim off 1/4"

2 3/4" x 5"
64b
64a
Seam Line
64

Step 1. Join diagonal corner 64a as shown. DO NOT trim seam as darker color behind 64a will show through.
Step 2. Join Rectrangle, Unit 64b as shown. Press.
Step 3. Trim 1/4" from top and bottom of unit. Unit should measure 2 3/4" x 5" after trimming.

Making Unit 68. Make 1.

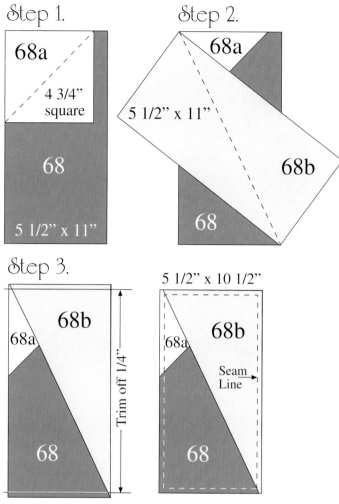

Step 1.

68a
4 3/4" square
68
5 1/2" x 11"

Step 2.

68a
5 1/2" x 11"
68b
68

Step 3.

68b
68a
68
Trim off 1/4"

5 1/2" x 10 1/2"
68b
68a
Seam Line
68

Step 1. Join diagonal corner 68a as shown. DO NOT trim seam as dark fabric behind 68a will show through.
Step 2. Join Rectrangle 68b as shown. Press.
Step 3. Trim off 1/4" from top and bottom of unit. Unit should measure 5 1/2" x 10 1/2".

Kodiak Quilt Assembly
Making The Small Tree.

1. Join Unit 2 to opposite sides of Unit 1. Refer to the quilt diagram, and join the two mirror image Unit 4's together as shown. Join mirror image Unit 3 to opposite sides of combined Unit's 4; then add to the 1-2 combined units, matching seams. Join mirror image, Unit 5 to opposite sides of Unit 6. Join to the tree bottom, again matching seams. Join mirror image Unit 7 to opposite sides of Unit 8; then add to the top of the tree. Join the two mirror image Unit 9's as shown. Join to the top of the tree; then add Unit 10 to the combined Unit 9's. Join Unit 11 to the right side.

Kodiak Quilt Assembly
Making The Bear & Tree.

1. Beginning with the bear, join units 12 and 13; then add Unit 14 to the right side of these combined units. Join units 15 and 16; then add Unit 17 to the top of the 15-16 combined units. Join these combined units to the right side of combined units 12-14. Join Unit 18 to the top as shown. Join units 19 and 20; then add Unit 21 to the top of the 19-20 combined units. Join these units to the top of the bear; then add Unit 22 to the left side, and Unit 23 to the right side to complete the front of the bear.

2. For the back of the bear, join units 24 and 25. Join units 26 and 27; then add them to the top of combined units 24-25. Join Unit 28 to the back of the bear. Join units 29 and 30; then add Unit 31 to the top of these combined units. Join the 29-31 units to the top of the bears back; then add Unit 32 to the right side. Join the back of the bear to Unit 23.

3. For the tree, join mirror image Unit's 34 as shown; then add Unit 33 to the left side of the combined 34 units, and Unit 35 to the right side. Join units 36, 37, and 38 in a horizontal row; then add these combined units to the tree bottom. Join units 39, 40, and 41 in a horizontal row; then add to the tree, matching center seams. Join units 42 and 43 as shown. Join these combined units to the top of the tree.

4. Join the tree to the top of the bear, matching the trunk seams. Join the bear/tree combination to the right side of Unit 11 to complete this part of the bear/tree section.

Completing The Meadow Section.

1. Join the two mirror image Unit 45's as shown; then add mirror image Unit 44 to opposite sides of the combined 45 units. Join Unit 46 to opposite sides of Unit 47; then add these units to combined units 44-45, matching the center seams. Join Unit 48 to the left side of these combined tree units, and Unit 49 to the right side. Join this section to the bear/tree section.

Making The Mountains.

1. Beginning on the left side, join mirror image Unit 64's as shown, matching all points. Join Unit 65 to the bottom of these combined units, and Unit 66 to the top.
2. Refer to page 124 for making Unit 62. Join Unit 63 to the top of Unit 62. Join these combined units to the right side of combined units 64-66, matching Unit 62c and 65 seams.
2. For the tree top, join mirror image Unit 51 to opposite sides of Unit 50. Join mirror image Unit 52's together as shown; then add to combined 50-51 units. Join Unit 53 to the left side; then add Unit 54 to the right side.
3. Join units 55 and 56. Refer to page 124 for making combined units 57-61. Join these combined units to the right side of combined units 55-56, matching points. Join these combined mountain units to the top of the tree section; then add this section to the right side of combined units 62-66.
4. Join units 67 and 68, matching mountain top points; then add Unit 69 to the top. Add these mountains to the right side of the other mountains to complete the mountain section. Join this section to the top of the bear/tree section, matching Unit 47 and 50 seams. Join Unit 70 to the bottom of the bear/tree section to complete the center scene.

Bear Paw Borders.

1. Join units 73 and 74. Make 2. Referring to the top border, join Block A to the right side; then add Block B to the left side Join units 71 and 72. Make 8. Join these combined units to opposite sides of the bear paw blocks as shown. Make two of these borders. One for the top of the quilt, and one for the bottom. Join the borders to the top and bottom of the quilt, referring to quilt diagram for correct position of bottom border.
2. For the side borders, join units 75 and 76. Referring to the left side border, join Block B to the top of the 75-76 combined units, and Block A to the bottom. Join previously pieced combined units 71-72 to opposite short ends; then add Block C as shown. Make two of these borders.
3. Join the borders made in Step 2 to opposite sides of the quilt top, matching seams where necessary to complete the quilt top.

Quilting And Finishing.

1. Mary's quilting has made this quilt into an art piece. The sky background behind the mountains was stippled with a swirl stippling stitch, and white thread. The snow capped mountain tops were quilted with curved lines in contour to the peaks. The mountains were quilted with gold metallic and curved lines that again were contoured to the mountains.
2. The meadow background was stippled using a swirled stitch and olive thread. The tree limbs were stitched with a gold metallic and a curved stitch. Again using gold metallic, the tree trunks were quilted with straight lines that curved occasionally for knots in the tree trunks.
3. The bear was worked with small swirls that resemble fur, in gold metallic. The inside darker blue border was quilted with diagonal lines and a dark blue thread. The medium blue border was quilted with straight lines going around the entire border. The bear paw blocks have three large gold metallic swirls, and the claws were "ditched."
4. Use five 2 1/2" wide strips for binding. Refer to page 13 for making straight-grain, French Fold binding.

Ask for more Leisure Arts/Pam Bono Designs books wherever quilting books are sold.

The Big Book Of Quick Rotary Cutter Quilts.
Quilts a la Carte.
Dear Pam....Teach ME Your Quick Quilting Techniques.
Pieces Of Baltimore....The Ultimate Collection.
It's Not Just Another Cover-Up!

www.leisurearts.com • www.pambonodesigns.com

For more of the joy to be shared with our gorgeous cover model, visit her on the internet at: www.zeldawisdom.com